In the Boojum Forest

Also available from Evertype

Murder by Boojum: A Mystery in Eight Fits
(Written and illustrated by Byron W. Sewell, 2014

The Aventures of Alys in Wondyr Lond
(Middle English verse by Brian S. Lee,
illustrated by Byron W. Sewell, 2013)

Alice's Bad Hair Day in Wonderland: A Tangled Tale
(Written and illustrated by Byron W. Sewell, 2013)

Snarkmaster: A Destiny in Eight Fits
(Written and illustrated by Byron W. Sewell, 2012)

The Haunting of the Snarkasbord (Alison Tannenbaum,
Byron W. Sewell, Charlie Lovett, August A. Imholtz, Jr., 2012)

Alice's Adventures in an Appalachian Wonderland
(Written and illustrated by Byron W. Sewell, 2012)

Álopk's Adventures in Goatland
(Written by Byron W. Sewell, illustrated by Mahendra Singh, 2011)

Alix's Adventures in Wonderland: Lewis Carroll's Nightmare
(Written and illustrated by Byron W. Sewell, 2011)

The Carrollian Tales of Inspector Spectre
(Written and illustrated by Byron W. Sewell, 2011)

In the Boojum Forest

A Portmanteau inspired by Lewis Carroll's
The Hunting of the Snark

by Byron W. Sewell

ILLUSTRATED BY
THE AUTHOR

2014

Published by Evertype, Cnoc Sceichín, Leac an Anfa, Cathair na Mart, Co. Mhaigh Eo, Éire. *www.evertype.com*.

A catalogue record for this book is available from the British Library.

ISBN-10 1-78201-078-5
ISBN-13 978-1-78201-078-4

Typeset in De Vinne Text, Mona Lisa, Engravers' Roman, and *Liberty* by Michael Everson.

Illustrations: Byron W. Sewell.

Cover: Michael Everson.

Printed by LightningSource.

Foreword

Byron Sewell has been writing or illustrating—or writing *and* illustrating—works inspired by Lewis Carroll's *The Hunting of the Snark*[1] for decades. Most of these were issued in very small limited distributions to his Carrollian friends and were never properly published. One early exception was his illustrated edition of *The Hunting of the Snark*, published by Catalpa Press of London in 1974. In 2012 I published some of Byron's more recent work along with some of his illustrations in *The Haunting of the Snarkasbord*,[2] together with a short piece entitled "Forks and Hope". I also published part of Byron's "Millennium Trilogy", which was written in 2000. This was *Snarkmaster*,[3] which Byron also illustrated.

This present volume publishes another part of "Millennium Trilogy", namely "In the Boojum Forest", a novella written in 2006, along with a shorter novella "Atchafalaya Boojum" and its even shorter sequel, "Blue Boojum" (2005), as well as a charming piece callled "Southern Fried Snark" (2005).

---

1 The publisher quite naturally recommends the Evertype edition, published in 2010 (ISBN 978-1-904808-36-7)

2 *The Haunting of the Snarkasboard* (ISBN 978-1-904808-98-5)

3 *Snarkmaster: A Destiny in Eight Fits* (ISBN 978-1-78201-002-9)

Many of Byron's works, both Snarkian and Alician, are set in locations where he has either lived or visited. A year living in Australia—where he illustrated *Alitji in the Dreamtime* (1975)—explains his interest in the South Seas and is part of the inspiration for *Snarkmaster*. Byron was born and reared in the Southwest, which explains his inspiration and interest in the themes of "In the Boojum Forest". He lived for a year in Kenner, Louisiana, near to the Atchafalaya Swamp, which gave rise, in part, to "Atchafalaya Boojum".

Some comments on Byron's illustration for the cover of this present volume may interest the reader. The Bellman and his crew have been searching for snarks in the midst of the famous Boojum forest in the desert climes of Baja California. Byron's attire for the Bellman is appropriate desert gear (in the style of Roy Rogers' sidekick, Gabby Hayes). He carries a pitchfork and is ringing his bell as a warning to his crew that he has encountered a rattlesnake. On the left-hand side of the back cover can be seen in the distance a small mesa that in reality is located a few miles south of Tucumcari, New Mexico, where Byron was born in 1942. In case you've missed it, there is a rather obvious visual puzzle in the illustration.

I am pleased to tell fans of Byron Sewell's sometimes violent, amusing, and eclectic Carroll-inspired tales that Evertype plans to publish many of his Alician fantasies and parodies in due course. Some of these were co-authored or inspired by Byron's own famously humorous sidekick, August A. Imhlotz, Jr.

The third part of the "Millennium Trilogy", the tale of a serial killer who murders some of the crewmen in a secret Snark Club in California, has also been published in 2014 as *Murder by Boojum*.[4]

Michael Everson
June 2014

4 *Murder by Boojum* (ISBN 978-1-78201-079-1)

Contents

Atchafalaya Boojum

"How doth the little crocodile,
Improve his shining tail,
And pour the waters of the Nile,
On every golden scale!

How cheerfully he seems to grin,
How neatly spreads his claws.
And welcomes little fishes in
With gently smiling jaws!"

—Alice's Adventures in Wonderland

"The fifth is ambition. It will be right
To describe each particular batch:
Distinguishing those that have feathers, and bite,
From those that have whiskers, and scratch."

—The Hunting of the Snark

CHAPTER I

Cocodrie

Georges LeBlanc poled his flat-bottomed boat slowly up the bayou as quietly as he could manage. His neighbour and fishing buddy, Mathieu Gaudet, sat up at the front, aiming the beam from a handheld spotlight that they had hooked up to a 12-volt car battery. They were searching for the tell-tale bright eyes of *cocodrie,* as they called alligators, which might be lurking in the water hyacinth. There was a thin slice of moon just above the horizon, but its faint light didn't penetrate into the dark backwaters and branches off of the big bayous. The particular backwater they were on at the moment was some ten feet wide and was relatively deep. Its low banks were overgrown with thick brush and trees, some of which bent so far over that their tops dipped into the water, their washed-out roots unable to hold their trunks upright. Every once in a while a snake would drop from a branch with a soft splash and swim silently away into the darkness ahead of them. The swamp was surprisingly noisy from the calls of frogs hiding in the trees or perched on the thick water hyacinth and lily pads.

The high intensity beam of the spotlight made it obvious that the heavy, musty air was aswarm with mosquitoes and other insects. Georges and Mathieu had put on so much repellent that the *cocodrie* could probably smell them coming. Still, it didn't do them all that much good; the hungry bugs bit them anyway.

So far, it hadn't been a good night for hunting *cocodrie.* They had seen a few small ones, not worth the trouble of shooting with the .22 rifle they carried in the boat. You could get a dollar for a small alligator skull, which sold well to tourists in the curio shops in New Orleans, especially to little boys, but it was messy work cleaning and bleaching them and there was a limit to what a person would do for a buck. However, there was real money to be made from the bigger alligators that were four to six feet long, and both Georges and Mathieu considered them to be good eating as well, especially deep fried in a fiery mustard and Tabasco batter. Catching one that big would make their night's efforts well worthwhile.

A sudden, very loud splash a short distance ahead startled them both, and Georges instinctively jammed the long pole into the thick mud to slow their boat.

"*¿Que diablo?*" Georges exclaimed.

Mathieu aimed the bright light in the direction where the noise had come from, but the beam hit the overhanging branches and only penetrated a short distance. "I'm not sure," he said, the tone of his voice revealing that he had been badly startled. "Something *really* big hit the water up ahead of us."

"What could be that big?"

"I dunno; maybe a panther fell out of a tree."

"Not likely. I been in these swamps all my life and I ain't never seen a panther."

"Oh, they're in here all right. I've heard other people say they've seen em. I heard one scream once."

"Well, if it's a panther, I sure don't want it leapin in the boat with us! Let's pull back to more open water."

"Now wait just a minute," Mathieu said. "If we leave, we'll wonder for the rest of our lives what it was; might be a big *cocodrie*," he suggested.

"How big?"

"I dunno; maybe ten or twelve feet. That could really be worth something!"

"How we goin to get anything that big back, even if we *could* kill it? We couldn't even get it in the boat; it'd probably sink it!"

"We could tie it up to a tree and go back for my power boat, then come back and fetch it. We could even tow it alongside if need be. We wouldn't have to get it into the boat with us."

"How much you think we could get for one that big?"

"It might fetch $500; maybe even more."

Just then the entire surface of the water around the boat vibrated intensely from a spooky low frequency noise that caused the bottom of their aluminium boat to hum, as if it had been touched by a tuning fork.

"*Mon Dieu!* You ever hear or feel anything like that before?" Mathieu asked, suddenly very afraid again.

The vibrations suddenly stopped, as if someone had tripped off a power switch.

"No, but I seen something like it once on a nature show on TV. A big bull *cocodrie* makes a noise like that when it wants to mate. That sound can travel for miles underwater and attracts females. It makes the water dance all around him when he does it."

"And probably attracts his rivals, too."

"Yeah; them too. If another bull responds there's usually a terrible fight for mating rights."

"You think that might happen here?"

"Maybe. Worse yet he might think our boat is another big bull."

"Oh, great! That's all we need."

"Don't get too upset. I got my pistol." Georges patted the handle of the .44 magnum he carried in a holster on his hip. "I don't care if that *cocodrie* is fifteen feet long; this pistol's able to crack an engine block at fifty feet. Any *cocodrie* sticks his head up where I can see it is goin to have a splittin headache for his last memory." He took the pistol out of its holster.

Suddenly the water all across the width of the bayou vibrated again, this time with more energy. They could clearly see beads of water lift into the air and dance across the vibrating surface like water hitting a frying pan full of hot grease.

"That SOB must be right under us!" Mathieu said, his voice revealing genuine terror at the possibility.

"Shine your light down here into the water," Georges said, pointing at the water beside their boat with the barrel of his pistol. "Let's see if we can see anything."

Mathieu aimed the spotlight at the water, but the beam could only penetrate a few feet into the murky pea green water. It didn't reveal so much as a perch. "Nothing!" Mathieu said. Georges moved the beam around, scanning the water across the width of the bayou. Suddenly a dark shadow in the water, as big as a pickup, rushed by, less than five feet away from the boat, travelling fast in the direction they had come from, as if trying to cut off their escape.

"You see dat?" they both asked each other in nearly perfect unison.

"Looked like a killer whale!" Georges said, in utter disbelief. "I saw something like that at Sea World in San Antone once. You'd see this dark shadow moving fast through the water, then the killer whale would come clean up out of the water, then belly flop. Looked just like that!"

Mathieu urinated in his pants.

"We've got to get out of this boat! Right now!" Georges said as he shoved his pistol back in its holster and frantically poled the boat over to the bank.

"*Vite! Vite!*" Mathieu was yelling, urging him on.

They were out of the boat in a few moments, grabbing at low limbs to keep from going deep into the water, and searching with their feet for underwater logs or cypress knees to stand on.

They were only a few feet back into the trees when they felt a rush of air, as if something huge had breached, followed momentarily by a loud, crunching splash as it landed square on top of their boat. A sheet of water cascaded over them through the surrounding trees. They both screamed instinctively, unable to control their own voices in this moment of panic.

Everything in the surrounding swamp went silent, except for the sound of water dripping from the trees. Even the frogs had momentarily stopped croaking. Then the ankle-deep water they were standing in vibrated again, and this time they could feel it on their boots and legs.

"Let's get back into them taller trees!" Georges said. "It likely can't follow us back in there."

"There's snakes in there!" Mathieu said, hesitating.

"To hell with the snakes! We've got a lot better chance against them than against whatever that thing is!"

They frantically fought their way through the tangle of brush and vines until they reached a small island of mud and moss, with a cypress rising up out of the middle. "Let's get up in this tree!" Georges said. "Here; I'll give you a boost up to that first limb and you pull me up after you. *Vite!*"

In a minute they were heading up the tree like black bear cubs, climbing as high as they dared, and both nearly out of breath, gulping the heavy, humid air, their hearts pounding.

Then they heard it come up out of the bayou and make its way towards them. Its steps made a sucking sound as its feet lifted out of the thick mud. Then it roared, or rather screamed; it was hard to describe. It sounded like it was directly below them, at the base of the tree. Georges and Mathieu both took death grips on the tree trunk, not sure what to expect.

"*Mauvais!*" Mathieu said through clenched teeth.

That's when it hit the tree. It felt as if a car had rammed it, and it was all they could do to hold on and not be knocked from their precarious perches. Georges decided that it was time to do something and pulled out his pistol. He fired three random shots towards the base of the tree, not able to see what he was shooting at it in the pitch-blackness.

This caused another terrible roar, this time from directly below and then they heard it retreat back into the bayou. A few minutes later the swamp reverted to its normal background noise of croaking frogs and buzzing insects. The smell of gunpowder was heavy in the thick, motionless air.

They stayed in the tree all night and until well into midmorning, afraid to descend, even though they could clearly see the ground now and that there was nothing waiting for them. "Well, we can't stay up here for days," Georges said. "I don't want to spend another night up here. And anyway, we'll eventually starve if we don't get back. We're going to have to try to work our way over to the main channel and see if we can flag down a fishin boat."

Mathieu knew he was right, but dreaded going back down, still terrified at what might be lurking below. Georges led the way and dropped down into the muck. Mathieu was soon down beside him. "Let's see what's left of our boat," Georges suggested. "I'd like to get a life vest if I can find one. I don't like the thought of drownin out here."

"What if it's still there? Just waitin for us to return?"

"Come on! It's a night creature. It's not going to expose itself like that. We're safe enough. And anyway, I can see to shoot now, and I've got three rounds left."

They made their way back to where they had come from, looking ahead for any sign of the creature's footprints, but the water had swallowed up any such evidence hours ago. They found what was left of their boat, smashed almost beyond recognition, half out of the water and half up against a tree. It looked like it had been through a hurricane. "Look at this! Can you believe it?" Georges asked.

"It's a damn good thing we weren't in it!"

"I reckon. We'd have been dead in an instant!"

They looked around for debris from the boat. Their ice chests were shattered and pieces were floating along the bank. However, their life vests were intact, having survived the impact better than anything else. They retrieved them and put them on, even though they were wet.

"Come on, let's get the hell out of here, just in case that thing hears us," Mathieu pleaded.

"Okay," Georges agreed. "We'll go back into the swamp a ways and try to follow along the edge of the backwater till we hit the main bayou." He thought for a minute, then said, "Look; we can't never tell nobody about this. We'll become the laughin stock of the parish. Probably lose our jobs and have to move away. Folks'll say we was attacked by the Boojum. We'll never hear the end of it."

Mathieu nodded. "I reckon you're right. No point anyway. Iffen I heard about it, I wouldn't believe it neither, so I don't figure anybody else would. What we goin to say happened to us?"

"We'll just say we rammed our boat on a snag and it sank. No one's ever goin to find what's left of our boat back in there. Who's goin to know or care?"

Mathieu nodded. "It'll be our secret. But I'll tell you this; I ain't never comin back out here into these deep swamps at night again. No way!"

"Me either. I'm goin to switch to bass fishin out on wide-open lakes in the daylight."

Mathieu nodded. "Georges, you know something?"

"What's that?"

"I don't believe that was any big *cocodrie*."

"No, me neither. I've heard big bulls bellow, and they don't sound nothin like that scream we heard last night."

"No, that weren't no *cocodrie* gruntin!" he agreed. "That sounded more like something straight out of Hell."

"Or the movies. Reminded me of *Jurassic Park*."

"Yeah; more like that."

"That's something else I ain't never goin to do again."

"What's that?"

"Watch them damn *Jurassic Park* movies."

"Yeah; me neither; too realistic!"

"Yeah!"

It took them several hours of struggling through the swamp to finally reach the main channel. Three hours later a boat finally approached and they started yelling their heads off to attract attention.

Dave Thibodeau pulled his bass boat up alongside the trees where they were perched like egrets.

"Thank God you heard us!" Georges said. "We wrecked our boat. We need a ride back into Morgan City."

"You want *me* to take you?"

"Yeah. We've been out here all night."

"I look like a taxi to you?"

"Well, no. But we really need help."

"I been out on a rig for two weeks. I just finally got here to do a little fishin. If you think I'm going to spend the next two hours takin you two idiots back to Morgan City you're crazy."

"We'll pay you."

"How much?"

Georges thought for a moment. "Fifty dollars."

Dave laughed. "Hell, I make that much in thirty minutes out there on that rig."

"Okay, then. How much you want to do it?"

Dave thought for a moment. "Five thousand dollars," he told him with a straight face.

"Five thousand dollars?"

"That's what it would take for me to throw away my day runnin you two up and down the bayou."

George turned to Mathieu. "How much money you got?"

"On me?"

"No, in the bank."

"Last I checked I think maybe I had $300."

"I only got $1,500." He turned back to Dave. "We only got $1,800 between us."

"Then you're up the bayou without a boat *or* a paddle," Dave said. "Looks like you two are goin to have to wait for the next bus."

"You don't mean that you're goin to just leave us out here, do you?" Georges asked is disbelief.

Dave didn't even bother to answer him, but revved up his boat and pulled away.

"Can you believe that son of a bitch?" Georges said. "You should have shot him."

"Yeah, I probably should have. But I'd rather save the bullet for that thing that tried to eat us, just in case it's been trackin us."

It was two hours before another guy in a boat finally saw them and picked them up. He didn't demand a fare.

Chapter II

Gray's Bayou

Dallas "Tizzy" Tizzard and his three companions approached the funky Boojum billboard as they drove west from Gibson towards Morgan City, heading for the boat launch, where they would put their bass boat into the Atchafalaya. "ST. MARY'S PARISH / HOME OF THE BOOJUM!" the sign announced. The faded sign needed a new coat of paint. The rain, sunlight and salt air had taken a heavy toll. Whoever had painted the sign had imagined the parish's legendary monster as having the head of a T. Rex, the feathered body and wings of an enormous rooster, and the scaly legs of a giant iguana. It was really something to behold. Bigfoot and Nessie seemed a lot more plausible.

Tizzy laughed out loud as they drove past the sign. "That damn Boojum always gets me right in my funny bone!" he said, pointing at the sign through the open window. "It looks like it came right out of one of ole Colonel Sanders' nightmares!"

Tom Guppy, Alan Twardy, and Leon Rocheleau, his old high school buddies at Central Catholic High in Morgan City, laughed with him. It *was* an undeniably funny sight.

"Yeah," Alan added. "They could serve it at Kentucky Fried Boojum."

"KFB!" Guppy added.

"Original or extra crispy?" Leon asked, pretending to be the one serving at the counter. This made them all laugh again. Not that it was all that funny; they just liked being with each other.

"What would you do if you was to meet something like that thing out in the swamp?" Guppy asked Alan. They all liked Tom's last name so much that they had never called him by his given name.

"Get the hell out a there as fast as I could!" Alan responded without hesitation. "What'd you do, Guppy?"

"I'd take its picture and sell it to CNN for a hundred thousand big ones," said Guppy.

"Take a picture with what? You bring a camera?"

"Of course not," Guppy said. "I'm goin fishin, not takin wildlife pitchures."

"There you go; you might miss the chance of a lifetime cause ye're too lazy to bring along a camera!"

"I don't reckon the chance of us actually seein that creature's any too high," said Tizzy.

"No; bout as high as seein Godzilla squash the Huey P. Long bridge!" Alan said.

"I reckon," Leon agreed and laughed at the thought of Godzilla rising up out of the muddy Mississippi to terrorize the Baton Rouge rush-hour traffic.

"I don't know. Tonight might be just the night to see it. You read in the paper about them two missin fishermen?" asked Tizzy.

"No. What about em?"

"Their families reported them missin when they didn't come back from huntin gators last night. They still ain't found any sign of em. The Coast Guard and game wardens have been searchin for them back in the Bayou Cocodrie."

"Hell, they probably just changed their minds and went into the French Quarter and found themselves some girls. Lot more fun than shootin gators!"

"No, the paper said they was good Christian boys; don't drink or nothing."

"I don't understand how anyone could not want a beer now and then!" Guppy said. "What're you sayin? You think the Boojum ate em?"

Everyone laughed at this preposterous idea.

Tizzy grinned big and went along with the joke. "Maybe. You know the legend. That hungry Boojum comes up outa the swamp every couple a years and eats a few folks, then goes back to wherever it lives for another two years. Them boys might'a been dinner."

"Yeah, right!" said Guppy, not buying it.

"I can tell you ain't a believer in our famous legendary monster," observed Tizzy.

"Are *you*?" Guppy asked, a big funny grin on his face.

"No; but something happens out there in the swamp every couple of years, almost like clockwork; about Labor Day. That's just a little over a week from now, you know."

"People just get out there in the swamp and lose their bearins and get lost," said Guppy. "Or they have boat trouble, or run out of gas, or drown water skiin with the snakes. Lots of things can happen out there. Some people probably even get themselves murdered."

"I figure that's why the phone company invented cell phones," said Alan. "Some big ole swamp Boojum jumps out at you, you call in the Coast Guard; or a squadron of F-4s to drop napalm."

"Call them from where? Inside the Boojum's belly?" Tizzy asked.

"Well, no. I reckon, that'd be a mite late to go makin any 9-1-1 calls."

"Yeah. A mite." Tizzy laughed as he pulled into the narrow parking lot at the ramp and then backed the boat trailer into the murky water. His companions jumped out and quickly released the boat, then climbed aboard. Tizzy pulled the empty trailer out of the water and parked the SUV. There were about thirty SUVs and pickup trucks already there, most with empty boat trailers. Sometimes it seemed like there were more SUVs and pickups than cars in South Louisiana. He locked up and waded out to the boat and clambered in. His friends already had the outboard engine idling.

It was early morning, and the sun hadn't quite come up over the cypress swamps between there and New Orleans, off to the east. It was late summer and the morning was already hot. They set out south from Morgan City at full throttle, into the main channel that led to Sweet Bay Lake, passing the shrimp boats just coming in from a night out in the Gulf. They hadn't been on the water more than fifteen minutes when the sun came up, and the dark water briefly lit up like golden neon from the reflected sunlight. All four of them put on their sunglasses at the same time, as if saluting a superior officer. They kept to the western side of Sweet Bay Lake and turned up the Big Wax Bayou for a short distance until they came to the main fork that put them into Gray's Bayou.

The water in the bayou was so still that it looked like polished marble. Every few hundred yards they would scare up egrets, or sometimes even a scarlet ibis, from out of the dead top of a tall cypress or from a perch on an old log. The birds would fly ahead of them, often just above the water, a mirrored brilliance of white or red on the dark water. Turtles would sometimes slip off of fallen trees or almost submerged cypress knees along the banks as they approached.

It took them another fifteen minutes to spot the plastic jug they had hung from a low branch to mark the location of their trotline. Tizzy cut the throttle back and they glided quietly into a backwater branch overhung with tree branches. He slowed the motor to a crawl as they approached their first float, an empty plastic milk container on which they had spray painted a big red "X" to identify it as theirs. "Okay, boys; let's see what we got," Tizzy said.

Guppy leaned out and tugged on the line to test its weight. "Something big on this one!" he said. He quickly pulled it up, hoping that it wasn't a big snapping turtle or a gar. In a moment there was a nice four-pound channel cat swinging in the air, struggling hard against the hook. The blackish-green skin on its back was as shiny as if it had been dipped in cooking oil.

"All right!" Leon said. "*Numero uno!* That's a keeper." Guppy plopped it down inside the boat and Leon stepped on its bony, flat head to keep it from hooking him with its erect dorsal fin while he deftly removed the hook with a practiced hand. He tossed the fish into an ice-filled cooler. "I can taste catfish and hush puppies already," he said. The only thing he liked better than catfish was shrimp, any way you could fix them. Leon reached into an old Styrofoam cooler and produced a chunk of rotten chicken that they'd left out in the sun for two days to ripen, and re-baited the hook. Then Guppy lowered it back into the dark water. Leon rinsed the slime off of his fingers in the bayou.

They worked their way along the line, pulling up three more catfish of a similar size and one three-foot long gar, which they hit in the head with a hatchet to kill before throwing it back in the water for the *cocodrie* and turtles.

"What's that?" Guppy said as they approached the next float, pointing to something white snagged on the float just below the surface.

Everyone looked in the direction he was pointing. "Net it," Tizzy suggested. "Maybe we can use it for bait."

"Oh, shit!" Guppy exclaimed when he lifted the net up out of the water. "It's somebody's hand! It's still got a weddin ring on!"

Alan turned to the other side of the boat and vomited his grits over the side; a little breakfast for the perch.

"Now what?" Guppy said, holding the net at arm's length, as if he thought the severed hand might make a sudden grab for him like Thing from *The Addams Family*.

"I reckon we'll have to take it in to Sheriff Paquette," said Tizzy. "Might belong to one of them missin guys they're searchin for."

"I wonder where the rest of him is?" Leon said, looking around the boat and over to where the black water filled in around the base of the trees. Alan was still throwing up.

"I vote we don't stay around and try to find him," Tizzy said. "Toss them catfish in with the beer and we'll put the hand in there on the ice."

Leon quickly transferred the fish and Guppy dumped the hand into the box, then covered it with ice. You could see the white of the broken wrist bones. Tizzy swung the boat around and headed back towards Morgan City as fast as the boat would take them.

"I figure the Boojum ate him, and that's all that's left," Guppy said, with a Cheshire Cat grin spread across his face. He had recovered his sense of humour once they had gotten back out into Sweet Bay Lake, well away from where they had found the hand.

"Yeah, right!" Tizzy responded, but half-believed him. It was spooky out in the swamp when something had scared you like that, and he was anxious to get back to civilization. Alan had finally quit throwing up and was sitting up in the bow, as far away from the cooler as he could get, breathing the rush of humid air, and trying to resist the black nausea that kept trying to overwhelm him.

They went straight into town and over to the Parish offices. They had decided to leave the hand in the cooler. Tizzy held one handle and Leon the other; not that it was all that heavy. It was just that neither one of them wanted to carry it up close.

Sheriff's Deputy Maurice LeClaire was seated at the front desk. He looked up when they came in. "You boys bringin me a mess of shrimp?" He'd known the four of them all their lives, all the way through high school.

"We wish," Tizzy said. "You got a strong stomach, Maurice?"

Maurice considered that to be an ominous question. "You pull people out of car wrecks and you soon get a strong stomach, or else you go find a different line of work. What you got in there? You better not be bringin some dead animal or a snake in here. You do, and you'll all spend the night back there in one of them cells."

"Well, I reckon it's dead alright, but worse that any snake," Tizzy said, setting the cooler on the floor in front of his desk and lifting the lid up. Maurice put his hand on his pistol grip just in case something mean came flying out of the cooler. Some of these kids had a weird sense of humour.

He peered in. "All I see is ice," he said.

"You got a pencil I could use for a prod?" Tizzy asked.

Maurice handed him a ballpoint pen, and Tizzy used it to scrape the ice away to reveal the hand.

"Where'd you get that?" Maurice asked, quite taken aback by what he now saw in the cooler.

"Back in Gray's Bayou. We was workin our trotline and this thing was snagged on one of our floats. We figured it might belong to one of them boys you guys are lookin for."

"Could be. Don't touch it."

"No problem!" Tizzy assured him. "You can have the damn cooler, too. I ain't never puttin that back in my boat."

"Where's Gray's Bayou?" Maurice asked. There were so many bayous in the lacework of waterways that cut through the delta that it was hard to remember all of them, even when you'd lived your whole life in the area.

"West of Sweet Bay Lake. It joins the Big Wax Bayou."

Maurice nodded, remembering it now. "You boys excuse me a minute while I go radio the Sheriff." He got up and went back into a small inner office. He quickly related what had happened to Sheriff Paquette, then went back out to where the four boys were standing, well back from the cooler. "The Sheriff says he wants us to meet him down at the Coast Guard Station. They'll have a boat down there waitin to pick us up. You boys are goin to have to take me back out there and show us exactly where you found that." He pointed at the hand in the open cooler. He went over and covered it back up with ice and closed the lid, then phoned the State Police to make arrangements for them to pick it up to send to the lab. "Should be easy enough to identify who that belonged to; what with a complete set of fingerprints and a weddin band."

"How will we get back?" Tizzy asked, not at all excited about the possibility of spending all day out there with the police and divers poking around for a body, or what remained of it.

"You show us the spot and we'll get you right on back; probably by airboat or helicopter."

"All right!" Guppy said. "Ain't never got to ride in one of them choppers before."

"It's not a promise," Deputy Maurice told him, "just a possibility; don't get your hopes up."

They went back outside to the parking lot. "You boys follow me on down to the Coast Guard Station; there ain't enough room in my squad car for all of you."

They followed Maurice and parked their rig, taking up three spots. The sun was well up now and it was already in the lower nineties. The filthy water had a strong smell of dead fish and diesel as they made their way down to the dock. A large airboat was waiting for them, with a Coast Guardsman holding a map. They climbed aboard and introduced themselves to Captain David Hunka, who opened the map. "Can you show me about where you found the remains?" he asked.

The map was mostly solid green indicating a vast swamp and marsh, but crisscrossed with narrow blue waterways. Tizzy pointed at a spot on Gray's Bayou. "Okay. I'll get us as close as I can to that location, then you can lead us to the exact spot. You guys have a seat." He pulled out a two-way radio and repeated their destination. "There'll be several boats with police and divers that'll meet us out there," he said. "Cast us off, will you?" Leon untied the boat and pushed them a few feet away from the dock. The big engine revved up and they glided out onto the channel, where they were soon roaring through the waterway at breath-taking speed.

They were met by several other boats on Sweet Bay Lake near the entrance of Big Wax Bayou. It took their small flotilla only about fifteen minutes to reach the entrance to the backwater where Tizzy and his friends had their trotline. Tizzy signalled to slow down the boat and they eased up to about the spot where they had found the hand. "It was caught on our sixth float," Guppy said. "But it could've just floated in here, so no tellin where it came from."

"There's not much current back in here and the natural flow is back out to the bayou, so there's a good chance the body might be close by," Maurice said. He signalled for another boat to come alongside. "They found the hand in this area," he told them. "Try draggin through here first. We might get lucky and snag the body. If that doesn't work then we'll need a couple of your divers to go down here and take a look-see. We'll pull on back out of here and give you guys some room to work. Pull that trotline up so none of you get hooked."

They made their way back out to the channel and tied off to wait for the search effort to get on.

"I don't see no chopper," Guppy said, obviously very disappointed.

"It's probably workin over towards the swamps south of Amelia," Deputy Maurice said. "We had a report of some clothes in the water over there and they're checkin it out. That's where Sheriff Paquette is. We'll probably have to take you guys back in one of these boats. We'll wait awhile and see if they come up with anything."

"I should've brought a fishin pole," Tizzy said as he sat down and tried to get comfortable. "I'll be amazed if they're able to find anything in that water. You wouldn't be able to see more'n a foot in front of your nose down there."

"What if they come up on a gator in there? They's some right big ones back in these bayous. My Dad and I was out here when I was a kid and we saw a big one, that was maybe twelve feet long; a real monster."

"People don't see many that big these days," Maurice said. "Still, there could be one. They'll post a couple of guys on the boats with high-powered rifles to keep an eye out for them. I reckon they'll be safe enough from the gators. I'd be more worried about steppin on a big snapper, if it was me in there."

"Who are these guys that are missin?" Alan asked.

"Couple of boys from over towards Gibson. They got big families over there. Their wives have been callin me about every hour wantin to know if we've found their husbands yet."

"What do you think might of took off that hand?" Tizzy asked Maurice.

"Hard to say; but it ain't easy to cut off a hand like that, except with an axe or a chainsaw."

"Or maybe he got a little too close to a big gator," Guppy suggested.

"I doubt it," Maurice replied. "A gator doesn't bite things off like that. They'll just latch on to an animal and drag it under to drown it; must have been something else."

"Like what?" asked Leon.

"Oh, people try to dispose of bodies sometimes," said Maurice. "Cut em up in little pieces and dump them out here in the swamp, hopin the gators will eat them and get rid of the evidence."

"That's supposed to be what happened to Jimmy Hoffa," Alan said. "I heard the Mafia cut him up in little pieces and fed him to the gators down in the Everglades."

"I heard that, too, but I don't believe it. Most likely they put his body in the trunk of a car and had it smashed in one of them wreckin yards. The Mafia controls most of those in New Jersey and New York. That mushed up mess would have then gone into a blast furnace, and they'd have never found a trace. A lot more efficient that feedin the wildlife."

"You guys catch any fish on your trotline?" Maurice asked, trying to change the subject.

"Yeah, we pulled up three nice channel cats, and one fair-sized gar," said Leon. "We killt the gar and tossed it in for the turtles, so's they'd have something to eat besides our bait. Those divers in there will likely be findin that gar afore long."

"You don't eat gar?" Maurice asked, smiling.

"Well, I eat most things; but not gar. The dang things are all bones and taste too strong. I don't like my fish to taste *that* fishy; I like white meat if I can get it; sand trout or Jew fish."

"I caught a freshwater gar one time in a river in Texas," said Tizzy. "This Mexican feller I was with kept it; he said it made good soup; wouldn't let me throw it back. He scaled it and took it home for supper."

"I'd have to be damn hungry to eat gar soup!" Leon allowed. "Even with lots of Tabasco. I hope I ain't never that hungry!"

"It might not be too bad in gumbo," Guppy allowed. "You can put almost anything in that and it'll taste real good."

"I was over to the Shark Rodeo at Texas City once, several years back," said Tizzy. "I saw a saltwater gar big enough to eat a kid or a big dog."

"No way!"

"I'm tellin the truth. They were catchin all sorts of big fish out in Galveston Bay and bringin em in to be weighed. They'd string em up on telephone poles using electric hoists. They had half a dozen eight to ten foot sharks strung up. While we was lookin at em, a pickup drove up to the weigh station with this gar about eight feet long and at least two feet across his gut. It was about one third teeth. And it wasn't dead, even though it must have been out of the water for half an hour. They climbed in and hooked it with a steel cable and winched it up a pole. That dang monster kept floppin and twistin around, trying to take a bite out of anybody that got within reach. It was still floppin around when we left about thirty minutes later."

"I'd of liked to have seen that!" Guppy said.

"This guy who was there and lived over in Galveston said that the canals around some of them fancy resort homes down by the water's edge on the backside of the island have those big saltwater gar in them. People's dogs jump in there to fetch a stick or something and the gars hit them. He said they lose lots of dogs that way."

"You'd think they'd lose a few kids that way too," observed Alan.

"You'd think; but I've never heard of that. I guess you have to teach them to be careful and not to fall in."

"I know one thing, after seein the sharks they drug out of Galveston bay, I never want to go fishin out there," said Tizzy. "You fall overboard and there's some real monsters swimmin around with you."

"Big as Jaws?" asked Leon.

"Well, no; not *that* big. But for sure big enough to take off a leg with one bite."

"I don't recall hearin about any shark attacks down at Galveston," Maurice said.

"Maybe not; but if you'd seen the size and nature of them sharks and gars you'd think twice about going too far out in the surf fishin for bone fish or sand trout."

They went on talking about big fish to kill the time while they waited for the divers to finish their search. About an hour later a deputy pulled up beside them in a small boat to talk with Maurice. "All they come up with down there on the bottom was a baseball cap and two toes."

"Two toes?" Maurice asked, a bit shocked by the news.

"Yeah, a big toe and a middle one; they aren't sure which one exactly, or even if they're even from the same foot."

"You callin it quits then?" he asked.

"Yeah; they say they've searched everywhere. I think they swam about a hundred yards up and down the bayou. They've even searched back in the swamps on both sides for about fifty feet, in case something drug a body out of the water back in there to eat on. Nothing back there though."

"All right, let's head on back," said Maurice. "They got those toes in plastic bags and in ice?"

"Yeah, they're packed up nice in zip-lock bags."

Maurice told Captain Hunka that they were ready to leave and they were soon speeding back to Morgan City.

When they were back in the parking lot Maurice came over to the four of them as they were getting ready to get in Tizzy's SUV. "I'm goin to need to ask you boys to keep quiet about this for a while. Don't talk to anyone about what you've seen, okay? Let the Sheriff make any sort of necessary announcements."

"Why?" asked Tizzy.

"We don't want to panic everybody around here, especially seein as how the Shrimp-PetroFest is startin next week," Maurice explained. "We wouldn't want folks to think there's someone or something out there in the swamps killin people and cuttin em up in little pieces to feed the gators; wouldn't be good for attendance."

"I suspect you're wrong about that," Tizzy said. "If you made an announcement that the Boojum got hungry and ate a few more people you'd have so many sightseers in here lookin for it that you wouldn't be able to handle the crowds."

"Yeah," Guppy agreed. "Folks like that kind of stuff. You wouldn't be able to rent a boat around here for weeks, people out looking for the monster."

"Either way, it likely wouldn't be good for the festival. We'll let the Sheriff and the folks in charge of the festival make that decision. Can I count on you boys to keep quiet about this?"

They all reluctantly nodded. "I expect you won't be able to keep a lid on it for long, though," Tizzy said. "There's too many folks will have heard about it. There's your deputies and the Coast Guard guys. There's the divers. Then there'll be the State Police or whoever does the lab work on the bits and pieces. And then, of course, there'll be the family of the victim once you identify him. They're sure to raise hell, wantin you guys to find the killer; whoever or whatever it is."

"You're probably right," admitted Maurice. "Still, I'd appreciate it if you don't say nothin till there's an official announcement. It'll make my life a lot easier. As soon as news of this gets out there'll be everybody from CNN to reporters from the Baton Rouge *Advocate,* the Lafayette *Daily Advertiser,* and even the New Orleans *Times-Picayune* in here wantin to know about what happened, and whether or not anyone's seen a Boojum. It's goin to be a damn circus!"

"Okay," Tizzy said. "We'll keep it quiet." The other three nodded.

"What if someone does see a Boojum?" asked Guppy. "You'll have reporters in here from as far away as Beijing, Moscow and Rio de Janeiro. You'll even have National Geographic film teams, and the Sierra Club in here trying to protect it as an endangered species. You sure won't get any sleep for weeks; maybe months!"

"There ain't no such thing as a Boojum, and you know it!" Maurice said. "That's just something somebody on the town council dreamed up to pull in a few tourists."

"I don't know," Tizzy said. "About every two years people start disappearin out in the swamps around here. I think this fits the cycle pretty good."

Maurice just shook his head. "You boys just keep a lid on it for now," he said as he walked off and got into his squad car.

Sheriff Justin Paquette was waiting for him when Maurice got back. "What'd you all find back in there in Gray's Bayou?" he asked.

"More body parts. Two toes. And a baseball cap. It probably belonged to the same victim."

"That it?"

"That's it. They searched hard underwater for about a hundred yards up and down the bayou, and back into the swamps on both sides for about fifty feet."

"You think they might have overlooked anything?"

"Well, the backwaters got lots of water weed in it, so they might have missed something small, I suppose; maybe another little toe or an ear or something. They wouldn't have missed anything big, though; like an arm or a leg. Did the State Police lab techs show up and collect the hand?" he asked, looking around for the cooler.

"Yeah they came and got it about an hour ago. They're goin to drop by the missin men's houses and try to get some prints from their dirty dishes and their tooth brushes; that sort of stuff, so they'll have something to compare the prints against."

"Too bad they didn't find the whole body. I just hope that there aren't bits and pieces strewn all over the swamp and people keep findin them here and there."

"If they *are* strewn all over the swamp then the turtles and gators will soon take care of em."

"You find anything over in Bayou Cocodrie?"

"No; it was a waste of time. The families can't identify the clothes that were found, so it's likely they didn't belong them."

"How we goin to handle the press when it gets out that the hand and toes of one of these guys has been recovered?"

"We likely won't know if those bits belonged to them for another few days. We don't have to say nothing until the lab reports come back. If they don't belong to one of the missin then we can just keep it low-key and say they're still missin. and we're workin on some recently discovered evidence. We don't have to say what. I sure hope those pieces don't belong to them. The timin couldn't be worse, what with the festival openin next week."

"I swore Tizzy and his three buddies that found the hand to silence, at least until the papers get wind of it. You might want to talk with the Captain Hunka and see if he can get his men to keep quiet as well."

"I called him already, but it may be too late for that. Hard to keep something like this quiet for very long. It's pretty sensational."

He had no sooner said this than Claude Généroux of *The Atchafalaya Advocate* came in. "*Allo,* Sheriff," he said. "Maurice."

"*Allo,* Claude. What can we do for you?"

"I hear someone found a severed hand out in the swamp this mornin."

"Now who told you that, Claude?" Justin asked.

"An anonymous source; he didn't give me his name, and I didn't ask for it. Any truth in it?"

"We're not ready to say anything about any on-goin investigation. We're waitin for some lab results."

"So there *was* a hand brought in!"

"I didn't say that."

"But you don't deny it."

"Look, Claude. The Shrimp-PetroFest's this next week. You don't want to go spreadin panic about something you don't know anything about. Wouldn't be good for business. Lots of folks depend on that festival for a good chunk of their annual income. You wouldn't want all these folks mad at you for spreadin rumors and hurtin them would you? I mean, you might have to go lookin for somewhere else to live if you did something real dumb like that."

"I ain't goin to spread any rumors. That's why I'm here askin for confirmation."

"Like I said, I can't confirm anything just yet. We don't know exactly what happened."

"Well, just suppose, for argument's sake, that there *was* this hand brought in. What might be a reasonable theory to explain somethin like that?"

"I'm sure you've got a bigger and better imagination than I do."

"Well, I guess it could be a murder," he suggested.

"Yeah; or—just for argument's sake—maybe an industrial accident," Justin suggested.

"An industrial accident? Out in the swamp?"

"Sure. There's lots of oil and gas drillin goes on out there. You know that. Roughnecks get their fingers chopped off with some regularity."

"Yeah, but I've never heard of one gettin his whole hand chopped off."

"Now, Claude; I haven't said anything about a whole hand, now have I?"

"No; but you haven't denied it either; and that's what my source said it was. I tend to believe him."

Sheriff Paquette was silent.

"Okay," Claude said. "I don't want to cause no trouble for anyone; you or the Festival. Will you let me know when you plan on makin any public announcements? You do that and I'll wait."

"I'll let you know first."

"Okay. Deal." He turned to leave and then turned back. "You find anything over at Bayou Cocodrie? I believe you were out there lookin for two missin fishermen. "

"No, there was just some T-shirts; that's it. The family didn't recognize them. We're still searchin."

The next day Deputy LeClaire received the lab report from the State Police by FAX, and quickly read it over before taking it in to show Sheriff Paquette. It wasn't good news. He walked into his office without knocking, since he knew that there was no one with him. "The State Police report just arrived. That hand didn't belong to either Ledoux or Poirier." He handed the FAX sheet to the Sheriff over his desk.

"Whose is it then?"

"They don't know. It says they don't have any matchin prints on record."

"They're comparin DNA from the hand and toes to see if they're from the same person. No point in contactin the Ledoux and Poirier families till we know that. We'll likely be gettin a request for blood samples from their wives and kids pretty soon."

"*Allo,* LeClaire," came a shout from the front counter.

"Lemme go see who dat is," the Deputy said in his best Cajun accent. It was Claude Généroux. "*Allo,* yourself. What you need, *mon ami?*"

"You seen today's edition of the Lafayette *Daily Advertiser?*"

"No; I don't subscribe."

"There's an item here on the front page about that severed hand I asked you about; the one you didn't want to admit to havin."

"Lemme see dat." he said, reaching out for him to hand it to him. "There, on the lower right."

"Yeah, I see it."

BODY PARTS RECOVERED FROM GRAY'S BAYOU

LAFAYETTE (UPI)— An anonymous source close to a Morgan City Sheriff Department investigation has revealed that a severed hand was discovered Monday by fishermen in a backwater off Gray's Bayou, west of Sweet Bay Lake.

The remains have been sent to the State Police crime lab for identification. Speculation is that it might belong to one of two Amelia men reported missing Sunday: Émile Ledoux and Eugène Poirier.

The Coast Guard, Louisiana Game and Fish wardens, St. Mary's Parish police, and the Morgan City Sheriff's Department have been searching for the missing men for several days, without success, concentrating on the alligator infested swamps around Bayou Cocodrie.

These recent disappearances, along with the new grisly discovery, have renewed speculation that the St. Mary's Parish "Boojum", a legendary monster said to inhabit the swamps around Morgan City, has re-emerged to feed on hapless human victims after a two-year fast.

The disappearances of Benoit Girard and Eugène Giroux two years ago in the same swamps have never been solved. Local legend is that these two men were the last victims of the Boojum, up until these recent disappearances.

"Did they get it right?"

"Just a minute, Maurice. I need to consult with Justin."

He took the paper with him into the Sheriff's office and closed the door behind him. "Well, the severed hand's hit the front page over in Lafayette." He handed the newspaper to him. "Down on the right."

"Well, all hell's goin to start breakin loose around here now," he said after he had read the article. "I thought you swore them boys to secrecy."

"I did. I doubt it was one of them. More likely someone at the Coast Guard Station, I figure. Anyway, what's done is done. Claude Généroux wants confirmation about the story. He's not too happy about bein scooped by an out of town paper."

"There's no point in tryin to hide it any longer. I'll go out and talk with him."

"*Allo,* Claude. Maurice tells me you're lookin for confirmation of this story."

"Yeah. I feel like you didn't do me right on this one. I held back waitin for you to make a public release and you didn't do it. Now it looks like I don't even know what's goin on in my own backyard."

"I'm sorry. We aren't sure who leaked it. I reckon it'll all start comin out now. You can go ahead and confirm part of the story."

"Which part?"

"About findin the hand. But the lab report says that it didn't belong to either Ledoux or Poirier. The prints don't match."

"Whose is it then?"

"We don't know."

"You don't know, or you're not sayin?"

"We don't know. Prints from the fingers didn't match up with any prints on record."

"You owe me something more on this. What else can you tell me?"

"Well, you can report that the search around Bayou Cocodrie came up negative; all we found was just a couple of unidentifiable T-shirts."

"That it?"

Sheriff Paquette hesitated. "No. I guess you might as well know that police divers also recovered a couple of toes where the hand was found."

"What?"

"Two toes; one a big toe. The crime lab is tryin to determine if they belong to the same body the hand came from. They'll have to use DNA analysis to do that, so it'll be awhile before they know for sure."

"Anything else?"

"Only that we'd like for you to downplay the 'Boojum' thing."

"Was there any evidence of a monster?"

"Like what?"

"I don't know; big tracks or claw marks on the tree trunks; that sort of thing. Anything that might indicate that there was a big animal in the area."

"No, there wasn't anything like that."

"You sure? Or are you stonewallin me again because of the Shrimp-PetroFest?"

"No; I'm bein straight."

"Well, I'll report that you don't have any evidence for the 'Boojum', but the connection with it'll make good copy, and I'm not goin to downplay it any more than that."

"Well, there's freedom of the press, and I can't stop you. Just be careful you don't incite something. People start racin off out into the swamps day and night lookin for monsters and there'll likely be more dead and missin. If there is, there'll be blood on your hands; morally anyway."

"Yeah, I understand your concern. I'll keep the hype low and caution the readers about goin out into the swamps ill-prepared. I appreciate your tellin me what you have. I might be able to keep my job now."

"*Au revoir*," Sheriff Paquette said, then turned and went back to his office.

"*Au revoir*," he replied as he walked out the front door.

Deputy LeClaire picked up a copy of *The Atchafalaya Advocate* the next day to see what Claude had written. It was worse than he had dreaded. The front page had a headline story about the discovery of the body parts out on Gray's Bayou. There was an interview with the Ledoux and Poirier families, who were understandably still hysterical about their missing menfolk. But worst of all, they had included a big special center insert, titled "The St. Mary's Parish Legendary Boojum". This special section recounted the local legend of the Boojum that was said to live out in the swamps south of the city, and how it fed on hapless humans on a two-year cycle around Labor Day. This included a list of all eight of the missing persons that were thought to be the Boojum's possible victims over the last decade, along with what personal information was known about them, and a map of the swamps showing where they were last seen. There was also a reprinting of a large portion of Lewis Carroll's nonsense poem, *The Hunting of the Snark,* along with some reproductions of two of Henry Holiday's original illustrations. They had even included a large photo of the goofy sign east of the city that depicted what the St. Mary's Parish Boojum was supposed to look like. And, keeping his word, there was a small, boxed inset that cautioned people about the dangers of going out into the swamps looking for the monster without being fully prepared, with the headline: "DON'T BECOME THE BOOJUM'S NEXT VICTIM".

Deputy LeClaire went on into the office and took the newspaper into Sheriff Paquette. "You seen this yet, Justin?"

"No." He took the paper and started to read it. "Check out the center section."

Just then the phone rang and Maurice went to answer it at his desk.

"St. Mary's Sheriff's Department," he said in a neutral voice. "May I help you?"

"This is Rhonda Ledoux, over in Amelia. I'm Émile Ledoux's wife. I just read the paper and they say that my Émile has gotten hisself eat up by that Boojum monster!" She practically screamed the last sentence.

"Now, Mrs. Ledoux, you just calm yourself. I've read that newspaper and it doesn't say that at all. It just speculates about it. People like to read sensational stuff like that. There's not one lick of evidence that such a monster even exists, and even less that he attacked your husband. You cain't believe things you read in the papers. Don't you know that? You just put that paper to good use by lining your birdcage with it. There's a whole lot of folks still out there, night and day, lookin for your husband and his friend. I believe that they'll find them. You just got to keep your faith up and say your prayers. If we find out anything, we'll call you, first thing."

"Do you promise?" she asked, then sobbed.

"I promise. You'll be the first to know. Now you just keep prayin and ask the Blessed Virgin to protect them till we find them."

"I will. That's all I've been doin for three days and nights."

"*Bon*. You try to get some sleep, now, you hear?"

"Okay."

"*Adieu.*"

"*Adieu.*"

He went back into the Sheriff's office. "That was Rhonda Ledoux. She was real upset by the paper this mornin. I'd like to punch Claude Généroux in the nose for scarin her like that. She was convinced that the Boojum had eaten her husband!"

Sheriff Paquette shook his head. "I'd like to find the person that started this Boojum rumor and put him in jail for a few years."

The phone rang again, and Deputy LeClaire went to answer it. "St. Mary's Sheriff's Department," he said. "May I help you?"

"Hey, Maurice. This is Marcel."

"Marcel! What you up to?"

"Five foot four and hatin it," he said, then laughed. Maurice joined him. "What you got?"

"I'm callin from New Orleans. I thought you might be interested in what's in the *Times-Picayune* this mornin."

"I'm afraid to ask."

"Well, it's about that Boojum you all got stompin around the swamps down there. There's a local radio station here that's offering a $50,000 reward for verifiable evidence the monster exists."

"Oh, no!"

"That's what it says. It's got a pretty good-sized article, too; all about the legend and the supposed victims. You all might want to start makin preparations for a lot of craziness down there in them bayous. This ought to be the most exciting Shrimp-PetroFest yet!"

"We likely won't survive it," Maurice said. "We might have to call in the National Guard."

"Yeah; I reckon you might. Well, I got to go. I just wanted to tell you about that big ree-ward."

"Thanks, Marcel. You take care."

Marcel rang off, and Maurice went right back into talk to Justin, who was on the phone. He stood patiently and waited till he was through.

"Good news!" Justin said when he hung up. "That was Captain Hunka over at the Coast Guard Station. They just found those two missin boys out in the swamp. They'd run out of gas and got lost. Had to get under some trees so they wouldn't burn up. They spotted the empty boat from the air and sent in a rescue team. Just in time, too. They were badly dehydrated and ate up by mosquitoes. But they're expected to survive."

"Well, that's good news for sure!" Maurice said. "We could use some good news around here for a change. But you know how it goes."

"How what goes?"

"I'm afraid I got some bad news right behind it." Sheriff Paquette stared at him, afraid to ask what.

"My friend Marcel Gautreau just called me from New Orleans. He tole me there's a local radio station offerin a $50,000 reward for verifiable evidence of the Boojum."

The Sheriff let his head droop until it bumped against his desk. "Oh, no!" was all he could manage to say.

"My very words," Maurice said. "We're about to get invaded by Boojum hunters."

CHAPTER III

Cover Up

Game Warden Jacques Menard had spent most of the last two days scouring the interlacing waterways and bayous west of Sweet Bay Lake looking for any evidence of an accident that might be related to the severed hand that had been turned into the Sheriff in Morgan City. He had grown up in Morgan City and knew the wetlands as well as anyone in the area.

Towards late afternoon he headed up a dead-end branch off of Big Wax Bayou and came across the crushed *bateau* abandoned by Georges LeBlanc and Mathieu Gaudet. It was just as they had left it, except that their Styrofoam coolers had finally floated out into the main bayou and off towards the Gulf. He got in close and examined the boat and was able to determine the boat's registration number. He put on hip waders and went into the trees and looked around for any evidence of foul play, but found nothing at first. It was just when he had turned to leave that he spotted a shattered tree root that looked like it had a slug in it.

He decided that it was time to call in investigators, and went back to his boat where he radioed the Louisiana State Police. "This is Warden Jacques Menard. I'm out in the swamps west of Sweet Bay Lake, on Big Wax Bayou, where I've just found a crushed boat and evidence of what looks like a large calibre slug buried in a tree. I'd like to request a forensics team to come in here and check this out. I'll wait out in the main channel for you." He then looked at his global positioning satellite readout and gave them his precise location.

It took the first of the State Police about 45 minutes to arrive on an airboat. A powerboat showed up about thirty minutes later. Warden Menard showed them the tree root, and the investigating team set about to saw out the section of the root containing the slug from the tree to take back to the lab. They scoured the area for other evidence, but found nothing obvious that might be of benefit in an investigation. They then phoned in the boat's registration number and quickly determined that the owner was Georges LeBlanc. It took them only a few minutes to hook up ropes to the remains of the boat and drag it out into the main channel, where they lashed it to the side and covered it with plastic sheeting to take it back into Morgan City for examination.

A pair of detectives was sent out that evening to interview Georges LeBlanc at his home. Detectives Eugène Giroux and Alain Maisonneuve knocked on his front door.

Georges answered the door, his dog beside him, barking wildly.

"Georges LeBlanc?"

"Yes."

"I'm Detective Eugène Giroux and this is Detective Alain Maisonneuve of the Morgan City Police Department. We'd like to ask you a few questions."

"Just a minute," Georges said. "Lemme put the dog in the bedroom. He might try to take a piece out of your leg."

He reappeared momentarily, the dog's barking now muffled behind a closed door. Georges invited them into the living room and turned off the TV, which was tuned to a fishing show. His wife appeared in the door to the kitchen with a questioning expression.

"It's okay, Angela." Georges reassured her. "These men are from the police; they just want to ask me a few questions."

"About what?" she demanded.

"I don't know, *ma chère*. They haven't told me yet."

Angela frowned, but didn't say anything more, and went back into the kitchen. The delicious smell of red beans and rice filled the house. Georges and the detectives sat down on the couch beneath a framed picture of the Blessed Virgin holding a baby Jesus.

"Do you own a boat?" Giroux asked.

"Yes, sir."

"Where is it?"

"I wrecked it out in the swamp."

"When was that?"

"Last Sunday night. I was out hunting *cocodrie*."

"Do you have a licence to hunt alligators?"

"Yes, sir."

"May I see it, please?"

Georges went over to a table and got his wallet, from which he produced the licence. He handed it to him. "It's current," he said. Giroux looked at it then gave it back to him.

"How did you get back into town after you wrecked your boat?"

"Two fishermen picked me up and brought me back to Morgan City."

"What were their names?"

"François and Louis. I don't know their full names."

"Where do they live?"

"I didn't ask."

"What exactly happened to your boat?"

Georges was silent for a minute.

"Do you have something to hide?"

"No."

"Then what happened to your boat?"

"It sank."

"No, it didn't; your boat was found and is now at the State Police lab in Lafayette."

Georges was silent again.

"Were you alone when this happened?"

"No."

"Who was with you?"

"My friend Mathieu Gaudet."

"What is his address?"

"Why?"

"We'd like to talk with him to verify your story."

"He lives just across the street at 407."

"We'll talk with him later. Now, I need to know what happened to your boat. It's evident looking at what's left of it that it was crushed with great force. How could this have happened out in the bayou where it was found?"

Georges was silent again.

"You really need to tell us. If you have done nothing wrong there will be no repercussions. Do you own a gun?"

"Yes. Several."

"Did you have one with you when you had this accident in which your boat was destroyed?"

"Yes."

"What kind of gun?"

"A Smith & Wesson .44 magnum pistol. We also had a .22 rifle."

"Why would you need such a powerful handgun?"

"In case I encounter a really big *cocodrie.* Or something else that might want to harm me. You never know out there."

"Did you discharge this handgun at the site where you abandoned your boat?"

"Yes. How did you know?"

"You left a bullet in a cypress tree root. Did you fire this weapon at someone?"

"No."

"What then? You get real mad at that tree and try to kill it?" Alain tried to suppress a laugh.

"No. It's just that if I told you what happened then you wouldn't believe me,"

Georges finally said. "Try me."

"It's a real strange story. I know you won't believe it."

"I've heard some mighty strange stories since being a detective, I can assure you."

"Okay. Well, my friend Mathieu and I was out huntin *cocodrie.* We went up this bayou. Mathieu was holdin the spot, shinin it across the water to look for their bright eyes. Suddenly we heard a terrible noise up ahead of us. Mathieu shined the spot in its direction, but we couldn't see nothing because of the limbs hangin down in the water. Then the water starts to vibrate wildly. Little drops of water were bouncing all over, and the bottom of the boat started buzzin."

"That was probably just a large bull alligator," Eugène said. "Males make that noise when it's mating season."

"I know. But this was very powerful! Mathieu shined the spot into the water, lookin for some big *cocodrie,* but we couldn't see nothing. Then suddenly this shadow as big as a pickup passed by underwater, goin real fast. A minute later the water started vibratin again, but this time even stronger. Drops of water was dancin all over the width of the bayou. We got real scared and poled over to the bank and got out as quick as we could, heading back into the swamp. Then we heard this terrible noise as something crashed on top of our boat. We climbed up a cypress as fast and as far as we could. This thing that had crushed our boat came ashore, stalkin us. It rammed the tree so hard that we felt that we might fall out. I shot three times into the darkness at the base of the tree to try to scare it away. I must have hit it, cause it screamed and went back into the bayou. We stayed in the tree until morning, then came down and worked our way through the swamp to the edge of the channel. The fishermen finally rescued us several hours later."

"So, you think it was a gigantic alligator?"

"No way! I been huntin *cocodrie* all my life. I've heard stories from the old timers. This don't match. Its screams didn't sound nothing like a *cocodrie*. I've heard them. That's more like a deep gruntin, bellowin sound."

"What you think it was then?"

Georges was silent again.

"Well? I'm just askin your opinion. I'm not goin to arrest you or anything."

"I figure it was a Boojum."

"A Boojum?" Giroux asked.

"Yeah. That *zombi* that lives out there in the swamp and eats people once in awhile when it gits real hungry."

The detectives were silent, staring at him. "See, I told you that you wouldn't believe me."

"Well, you're right; it *is* just a bit hard to believe," Giroux said. "Tell you what. We're goin over to your friend Mathieu's house and see if he tells us the same story. We'll be back in bit." They got up and walked across the street to Gaudet's house. Mathieu grudgingly told them the same story, with just enough added detail to make it believable.

"Mathieu, I wonder if you'd mind comin with us back over to Georges' house for a few minutes?"

"I reckon I don't mind."

"Good."

They walked back across the street and knocked. Georges let them in and they went back into the living room and sat down.

"Now, we're goin to have to write something in our report," Giroux said. "I don't think we can write down that you boys were attacked by a Boojum. The papers would have a field day with that. You'd probably have to move to Godawful, Texas, to start a new life."

"What's your plan then?" Alain asked.

"Well, we can't deny the damage to the boat."

"No, that's true."

"I think what we should do is just say you boys told us that you were attacked by a very large alligator. How big a gator you figure it would take to flatten your boat like that?"

Georges thought for a moment. "Twenty, maybe even twenty-five feet, I reckon."

"What do you think, Mathieu? You agree that it would have to be that big?"

"Yeah; at least."

"Do they even get that big?" Giroux asked.

"None that I ever heard of," said Georges. "The biggest one I ever saw was when I was a kid was maybe fifteen feet long."

"How bout you, Mathieu. You ever heard of one gettin that big?"

"No. But there's lots of strange things out there in them swamps. It might be possible."

"All right, so in theory, one might get that big, if it lived to be 75 or 100 years old. I seem to remember that Australian saltwater crocodiles can get that big."

"At least the one in *Crocodile Dundee* got that big," Mathieu said, as if he believed it to be a true-life documentary.

"There you go!" said Eugène. "Lots of folks have seen that crazy movie. So, they'll probably agree that it's at least a possibility."

They all nodded.

"Okay. We're goin to put in our report that you were attacked by a very large alligator; perhaps twenty-five feet long. It smashed your boat and you had to run for your lives into the swamp and up into a cypress."

They all nodded. "If any of you ever change that story I will personally blow your head off. I won't take kindly to anyone sayin that I faked a report. My pension might be dependin on this." He said this with real menace and none of them doubted him for a minute. "If some damn reporters show up at your houses wantin to know what happened you tell them this story. I don't want to read anywhere that you think you was attacked by a damn Boojum. Clear?"

"Clear," said Georges.

"Clear," said Mathieu.

Giroux and Maisonneuve got up and left.

"You hungry, Mathieu?" Georges asked.

"Yeah; I'm always hungry."

"How's about some red beans and rice? Angela's cooked up a nice mess with some real good *andouille.* And I think she's been makin *beignet,* too! Go on home and get Dora and the kids. I'm sure we got plenty."

Chapter IV

Alan in Zombiland

Tizzy, Alan, Guppy, and Leon sat in the shade of a big oak tree in Lawrence Park eating mudbugs, drinking beer and listening to "Michael Douchet and The Cajun Swamp Snarks" playing their own version of Nathan Abshire's *The Good Times Are Killing Me.* A ten-foot high cutout of a shrimp wearing a hardhat and playing an accordion was mounted above the stage. Its tail had been mounted on a pivot and motorized with an electric motor and a V-belt so that it continuously moved back and forth, as if keeping time to the lively music. It was a fine, hot day, and there was a huge crowd of perhaps 10,000 people, most of them trying to squeeze in under the shade of the trees to get out of the direct sun. Rows of food stall awnings lined the edges, selling everything from Crawfish *Étouffée* to *Jambalaya.*

"I've been thinkin about that $50,000 reward," said Tizzy as he peeled another crawdad. "We ought to go back where we found that hand and have a better look around to see if there's any evidence of some sort of monster. That's a lot of money."

"Speaking of that, did you guys see that picture of a crushed boat in *The Atchafalaya Advocate*?" Guppy asked.

"Yeah; two guys claim a big gator smashed it," Alan replied.

"Said it was twenty or twenty-five feet long! Silliest damn thing I ever read. They don't get that big."

"They probably did before white men showed up and started shootin everything in sight," Alan suggested. "I'd sure like to see one that big."

"A gator would have to live a very long time to get that big," Guppy observed.

"I was thinkin that maybe that big gator's responsible for bitin off that hand we found; and them toes. Maybe those bits and pieces were sort of like the crumbs after its meal."

They were quiet for a moment as they each visualized this.

"Well, if that's what it was then it might be real dangerous to go in there lookin for it," Guppy said.

"We could each take a deer rifle," Tizzy said. "And pistols as backup," said Alan.

"What would we do if we found it?"

"Take some videos, I guess."

"What if the Radio station says that a big gator doesn't qualify as finding a Boojum?"

"We should call em and ask first," Tizzy said. "I'll do that."

"When you want to go?" Guppy asked.

"Let's go in the mornin."

They all agreed to meet at Tizzy's house. He got up and went to look for a pay phone while the others sat back and listened to The Cajun Swamp Snarks and watched the couples dance the Zydeco Two-step on the small temporary dance floor that had been laid out in front of the stage.

Tizzy returned fifteen minutes later, wearing a new T-shirt. It had "BOOJUM BLUES" across the top, with what looked like a dancing cartoon T. Rex playing an accordion below it.

"Where'd you get the T-shirt?" Guppy asked.

"They're sellin em in a booth over there."

"How much?"

"Fifteen dollars. I talked to the radio station. They said that if we can document a gator bigger than 20 feet in length in the swamps south of Morgan City that this would qualify. But they have to have hard evidence, preferably a dead alligator. I called the Department of Game & Fish. They said that as long as we have a valid licence we can shoot one as big as they come. But they laughed at the idea. They said they hadn't heard of one bigger than 16 feet since the early 1900s. They told me that if we did find one that big it'd be worth more alive than dead, but didn't think it would be too smart for us to try to catch anything that big and powerful. They strongly advised us to leave it alone if we found one."

"I vote we go for a dead alligator," said Guppy. "I like my hands and other extremities still attached to my body."

A loud round of applause went up from the crowd as The Cajun Swamp Snarks wrapped up their set. "Those guys were real good! Who's up next?" Alan asked. "It's supposed to be Wayne Toups," Leon said.

"When's Doug Kershaw playing?"

"Not till about four o'clock, I think."

"I need another beer," Tizzy said. "You guys need one, too."

They all allowed as how they did, and Tizzy made another beer run.

The following morning the boys were out on the water by seven o'clock, heading for their old trotline. They were armed to the teeth, looking like a small band of mercenaries setting off to topple some tiny fourth-world government. Tizzy pulled their boat up the backwater, recognizing their old marker, and tied off about a hundred yards back from where they had found the severed hand. He landed his crew with care, then handed each of them their rifle once they were safely on the muddy bank. He passed his own rifle ashore, then the camcorder and finally climbed out himself, managing to get pretty soaked in the process.

They spread out a bit, trying to find small clumps of grass and logs to walk on, and looking hard for snakes. They went perpendicular to the bank until they finally reached a small area of what passed for solid ground, though it was really just decades of grass that had packed down. It was eerily quiet, the frogs having all retreated to their daytime hiding places, and it was stifling hot. There was absolutely no movement of air in the grove of cypress and brush.

“I don’t see any tracks,” Guppy said.

“I doubt we’ll find any,” Tizzy said. “The ground’s too waterlogged. Let’s just look around for any areas where the brush and grass are pressed down, where something huge might have passed by. Let’s head over that way,” he said, pointing.

They were all eager enough and set out in that general direction. They slowly made their way for several hundred yards until they arrived at what appeared to be a cut through the brush that led down to the bayou.

“This could be something,” Guppy said, quite excited at what they were looking at. “It would be big enough for a large alligator to pass through.”

“Something’s obviously been through here,” Tizzy agreed. “The grass and weeds are all flattened and broken.” Tizzy turned on the camcorder and started to film the run. Guppy posed in the middle, acting like a great white hunter, posturing with his rifle.

Suddenly a loud guttural bellow came from somewhere back in the swamp directly behind them, and they all wheeled around.

"Run!" Guppy screamed, already moving back in the direction they had come from.

"*Vite! Vite!*" Leone yelled right behind him.

In a moment all four were rushing as fast as they could over the stumps and snags. Tizzy whirled around to see if they were being chased just in time to see a large bull alligator heading down the cut towards the bayou. He filmed it for a moment, then jerked up his rifle. "Shoot!" he yelled and then put two bullets into the alligator behind its front shoulder.

Alan was the only other one with enough presence of mind to turn and get off another shot. It struck the alligator harmlessly near the base of its enormous tail. The alligator collapsed and came to a rest.

They stood still, looking at the huge alligator for a minute, afraid to approach it. Finally Tizzy started to walk back, stopping every few steps to film it with his camcorder. Within a few minutes they were all four standing near the head, about ten feet back, studying the monster.

"Now what?" Guppy finally said. "What if it isn't dead?" Leon asked.

"It looks dead," Alan said.

The alligator took this as a cue and suddenly lurched forward a few feet, obviously not quite dead yet. They all four screamed and jumped back, then started laughing at themselves. Tizzy finally walked up and put two more shots into the alligator's head, right between its eyes.

"This is the biggest damn gator I've ever seen in my life!" Guppy said. "I just hope it's at least a twenty-footer." He reached into his pants pocket and pulled out a small tape measure. "Here, help me measure," he said to Tizzy.

They taped it off, from the tip of its snout to the end of its tail. "Eighteen feet, three inches," Guppy said, his voice heavy with disappointment.

"Damn!" Tizzy said. "There goes our fifty thousand."

"It might still be worth a lot," Alan said, "if we could get it back, but there's no way we're ever going to drag that thing out of here. We'd have to have winches."

"It probably weighs a thousand pounds."

"At least," Guppy said, who got down on his knees and put his shoulder up against it, fruitlessly tried to budge it.

"Let's go back into town and get help," Tizzy said. "I know this old guy named Gaston Arseneault who's hunted gators for forty years. I can probably get him to come out here and help us skin this thing. We could cut off its head and take it back. The skull and belly skin have got to be worth a bundle." Tizzy went up to the alligator's head and pulled open the enormous jaws to reveal an amazing set of eighty yellowed teeth, several of which had been broken in fights with other males. "First though, let's take some pictures. You guys all get up on its back with your rifles and I'll film you."

This seemed like a very good idea and they all clambered up, posing with their rifles. At which point the alligator lurched again, and all three jumped off and ran a short distance. Tizzy captured it all with the camcorder.

"Shit!" Guppy said. "I thought it was dead!"

"I'm going to start calling you guys Larry, Curly, and Moe," Tizzy said, laughing so hard that he had to hold his stomach.

The Three Stooges joined him in laughing at themselves. Tizzy sat the camcorder down on a log then went up and put another shot through the animal's head. "I wish I knew where this thing's tiny little walnut of a brain is," he said. "Don't keep pumpin shells into it. You'll destroy the skull and we won't be able to sell it for as much."

"I just don't want it to get up and slide into the bayou!" Tizzy said.

"It ain't goin anywhere," Alan assured him.

"All right. Let's head back and get help. One of you guys needs to stay here and guard it."

"No way!" Leon said with finality.

"Me neither," said Guppy. "You guys might not come back. That boat leaves, I leave."

"I'll stay," Alan said. "Leave me the bottled water, a life jacket, and a knife."

"Okay. It shouldn't take us more than three hours. Even if we can't get Gaston to help us skin it we'll come on back out and get you before dark."

"You'd better! I'm not going to be too happy if I have to spend the night out here with things like this monster roamin around lookin for supper." He kicked the alligator in the ribs.

Tizzy went back for the water, life jacket and knife, and picked up the axe for good measure.

When they were ready to go, Guppy went up to Alan and said, with melodramatic feeling, "Well, Alan, ole buddy, it's really been great knowin you!"

Alan didn't think this was all that funny, but Tizzy and Guppy thought it was hysterical.

"Don't worry," Tizzy told Alan. "We'll come back and get you; at least what's left."

"Ha ha!" Alan said, but wasn't smiling.

Tizzy, Guppy and Leon made their way back to the boat and set off for Morgan City to look for Gaston. Alan went over and sat on a log where he could look at the enormous alligator and take a drink of water. It hadn't moved now for about fifteen minutes, and Alan assumed that it had finally died, but he was still leery.

A wood duck suddenly winged through the trees with a rainbow flash of colour, startling him a bit. It was unbearably hot and there was no movement of air. But worst of all, the mosquitoes had found him. He got out the repellent and put on a thick layer and idled away the time by smacking the mosquitoes that landed on his jeans to try to bite him through the thick denim.

He didn't really hear the Boojum coming up behind him until it was less than twenty feet away. When he finally heard the wet sucking sound as it raised a hind foot Alan jumped up and whirled around, then froze, momentarily too terrified to scream or run. Recovering, he grabbed for the rifle propped against the log on which he'd been sitting, but the Boojum closed the gap between them before Alan could get the rifle up to his shoulder. The gun discharged harmlessly into the top of a cypress, knocking down a six-foot strand of Spanish moss.

The Boojum bit Alan's head off as easily as you'd pull the head off of a crawdad, and spit it out. It then ripped him apart and ate most of him. While this was happening the alligator recovered enough to get back up on its short legs and slide down the run into the bayou. In less than an hour there was essentially nothing left of Alan except his head. The Boojum retreated back into the swamp.

Two hours later Tizzy, Leon, and Guppy, accompanied by Gaston Arseneault, returned to find Alan's bloody clothes and his head, which seemed to be staring back into the swamp where the Boojum had gone. The grass around the log where he had been attacked was covered in blood and the swamp water itself had turned from pea green to blood red. Tizzy, Guppy and Leon ran into the bushes in three different directions and threw up. When he had recovered slightly, Leon went back to the boat, refusing to look anymore. Gaston, inured to the sight of blood from years of skinning alligators, walked carefully around the gore and over to where the huge alligator had been.

"Dis where dat *cocodrie* was at?" he asked.

Tizzy came over to him. "Yes. We shot it least six times. I even shot in three times in the head at close range; right between the eyes. I don't understand how it could have gotten up to attack Alan."

"Dem *cocodrie* is mighty tough, dat for sure. Strange though."

"What?"

"It bitin off his head like dat. I never seen dat before. *Mauvais, mauvais.*"

"Do you think it drug Alan into the bayou?" Tizzy asked, looking down the cut.

"No. Whatever killed your friend ate him right dere." He pointed to the spot.

"What do you mean? Are you saying that the alligator didn't eat him? That something else did?"

"Maybe." Gaston went back over to where Alan had been killed and walked a ways back into the swamp, studying the ground, with Tizzy and Guppy right behind him. Guppy was carrying his rifle at the ready, just in case something rushed them, though it was unlikely that he would have had the courage to stand and shoot if it charged. "Look here!" Gaston said, pointing to what resembled a very large footprint in the soft muck.

Tizzy and Guppy bent down to examine what he was pointing at.

"That's the biggest alligator print I've ever seen!" Tizzy said. "How big would the gator have been?"

"*If* dat *was* a *cocodrie,* maybe twenty-five feet."

"What do you mean 'if'?" Tizzy asked.

"Might not be a *cocodrie.*"

"Then what was it?"

Gaston shrugged his shoulders. "Maybe dat was a *zombi.*"

"A *zombi?*" Guppy asked. "You mean the living dead?"

"No, not dat voodoo stuff you see in movies. A *zombi* is a bad swamp spirit; a Boojum."

Tizzy and Guppy both straightened up and scanned the swamp, as if they might see it lurking there, hiding behind one of the big cypresses.

"Well, I think we had better go back and tell the Sheriff what's happened here."

"*C'est bon,*" said Gaston, quite happy to get away from this evil place.

"Should we take Alan's head with us?"

"No, do'n do dat," Gaston said. "De Sheriff will consider dis to be a crime scene; you do'n want to go touchin nothing. Leave dat rifle, too!"

Gaston led the way back to the boat. They all climbed in and sped back to Morgan City.

CHAPTER V

Tizzy's Tale

Sheriff Justin Paquette and his Deputy Maurice LeClaire sat in the sheriff's office watching Tizzy's home video for about the tenth time. "That's sure one hell of a *cocodrie!*" Justin said as he looked at the scene where Guppy, Alan and Leon were standing on the alligator's back with their rifles, clowning around and acting like great white hunters. If it wasn't for Alan's tragic death, the scene where the alligator moved and they all fell off would be worth sending into *America's Funniest Home Videos.* It would be sure to win the $10,000 prize."

"It must have been real bad to be attacked by that monster," Maurice said. "Makes you want to stay the hell out of the swamp!"

"No chance of that for us."

"I don't understand how they could have shot that thing five or six times with high powered rifles and it still be able to attack and eat Alan, then escape into the bayou."

"I figure it'll die eventually," Justin said. "From internal bleeding or infections."

"I hope."

Someone rang the bell on the counter out front and Maurice went to see who it was.

"*Allo,* Maurice."

"Claude! What's up?" Claude was also wearing a "BOOJUM BLUES" T-shirt. They were evidently selling well.

"I understand that there's a video of the big alligator that ate Alan Twardy."

"Yeah. Justin's back there lookin at it."

"Any chance I can watch it?"

"I doubt it."

"Would you mind askin?"

"Okay; I'll ask." Maurice went back to make Claude's request.

Justin came out to talk with him. "Claude," he said when he came up to the counter.

"Mornin, Sheriff. I was wondering if you might let me watch Tizzy's home video. That be possible?"

"I can't let you. Tizzy might though; it's his property. I'll be givin it back to him later today."

"You think that big alligator's dead?"

"I ain't got any way a knowin," Justin said. "But I hope it is. I'm gettin real tired of cleanin up after it."

"You think that gator was what folks call the Boojum?"

"Likely. I hope so anyway. I'd like for that legend to die."

"You goin to Alan Twardy's funeral this afternoon?"

"Yeah. Maurice'll be lookin after the store while I'm gone."

"What are they going to *bury?"*

"I believe they have cremated the remains."

Claude nodded. "Makes sense."

"You sure I can't take a quick look at that video?"

"You got to go see the Tizzards."

"Okay," Claude said, deciding it was best not to press the matter. "*Adieu.*"

"Take care," Justin said. "You stay out of dem swamps, hear?"

"No problem," Claude said.

The next day Claude went over to Tizzy's home and knocked on the door. His mother answered. "Yes?"

"My name is Claude Généroux from *The Atchafalaya Advocate.* I wonder if I might speak with your son, Dallas?"

"Just a moment," she said, but didn't invite him inside.

In a minute Tizzy appeared at the door. "You want to see me?"

"Hi, my name is Claude Généroux from *The Atchafalaya Advocate.* I wonder if I could talk with you for a minute."

"I reckon." Tizzy came out onto the porch. "Have a seat," he said, pointing to one of two plastic lawn chairs. Claude sat down in one chair and Tizzy sat in the other. "What is it?"

"I was wonderin if you could tell me about what happened out in the swamp that resulted in your friend Alan's death?"

"This for the paper?"

"Yes. I want to do an article. People are very interested."

"Well, we went out to see if we could locate the big gator that bit off the hand that we had found earlier in the week workin our trotline. We were thinkin about the $50,000 reward offered by the New Orleans radio station for evidence of the Boojum."

"But that was for a legendary creature, not an alligator."

"I called and asked them how big an alligator would have to be to qualify. They said if we found one over twenty feet long they'd give us the money."

"How big was the one you shot?"

"We measured it with a tape. Eighteen feet and three inches."

"So it didn't qualify for the reward."

"No."

"Why was Alan alone when it attacked?"

"We went back to Morgan City to get help from a gator hunter I know; to skin it. We figured the head and hide might be worth some real money. We left Alan to guard it."

"By himself?"

"Yeah. We thought it was dead anyway. That was a mistake. If there'd'a been two of us there he likely wouldn't a been killt. I blame myself. I feel real bad about that. Guppy and Leon feel bad, too."

"Guppy and Leon?"

"They were the other friends that were with us. Tom Guppy and Leon Rocheleau."

"Sheriff Paquette tells me that you took a video of the alligator, before you went back into Morgan City."

"Yeah. He brought it back yesterday. He'd borrowed it."

"I wonder if I might watch it?"

Tizzy thought for a moment. "I guess there's no harm. Come on in. I'll put it in the VCR in the den."

They got up and went into the den, where Claude watched it. It took less than five minutes."

"I wonder if I might have a still photograph of the alligator, with your friends standin on its back for use in the next issue of *The Atchafalaya Advocate*?"

"I'll ask Alan's folks if they think that's all right. If they say yes then I'll have one made and drop it by your paper's offices, if you'll pay for the cost."

"That would be fine. Do you think that this alligator was the legendary St Mary's Parish Boojum?"

"No, Sir."

His answer surprised Claude. "Really? Why not?"

"My friend, Gaston, who went back out there with us to skin the gator, found a big footprint back from where Alan was killed. He said it was too big to belong to a mere eighteen footer."

"A *mere* eighteen-footer? How big did he think it was?"

"He guessed maybe twenty-five feet."

"Twenty-five feet?"

"Yeah."

"There's never been one that big. I checked on the Internet. They don't get any bigger than six meters; that's about 20 feet. And they haven't seen one that big since the early 1900s."

"I know."

"Even the biggest crocodiles in Africa don't get bigger than seven meters. That's just twenty-three feet."

"I know. Scary thought, ain't it. Those African monsters can bring down a zebra or a wildebeest. I've seen it on TV. You goin to report that?"

Claude thought for a moment. "No, I don't think so. It's just speculation. Even if it's right, it would just result in hunters going back in there to find it. Someone else might get killed."

"Likely."

"Do you plan to go looking for it?"

"I don't know. I've thought about it."

"Wouldn't you be afraid?"

"Of course."

"How would you protect yourself?"

"I was thinkin about getting me one of them new .50 calibre rifles I've seen on the news. They can crack an engine block from a mile away. Fires a single .50 calibre machine gun shell. I reckon that ought to do the trick."

"They're very expensive."

"Yeah. About two grand, I think. It'd be worth it to kill that damn thing. And I can resell the gun after I'm through with it."

Claude looked at him for a moment. "I think if I was you I'd just let it be."

"Well, he wasn't your friend."

"No, he wasn't. Still, you might end up the next victim if you go messin with it."

"I don't think so. I know what I'm lookin for now; and I know about where to find it."

Claude thanked him and got back in his car. He drove over to interview Georges LeBlanc. Georges was out in the front yard mowing his lawn when Claude drove up. He parked his car in the driveway behind Georges' pickup and got out. Georges killed the mower when he saw him get out of his car.

"Good morning," Claude said as he walked over to him.

"Morning," Georges responded. "You sellin something?"

"No, no; nothin like that. Are you Georges LeBlanc?"

"Yeah. That's me. Who are you?"

"Claude Généroux," he said, extending his hand. "From *The Atchafalaya Advocate.*"

Georges shook his hand. "What can I do for you?"

"I read in a police report that you were attacked out in the swamp by a large alligator. I'd like to talk to you for a minute. I'm sure our readers would be very interested in hearin about it."

"I told the police all about it. I imagine it's all in their report, which you said you've read."

"Well, actually the report's a bit sketchy. All it said was that you and a friend," he looked at his notes, "a Mathieu Gaudet, were out in the swamp when you were attacked by an alligator estimated to be between twenty and twenty-five feet long. It destroyed your boat. You managed to escape and were picked up by fishermen, who brought you back to Morgan City."

"Yeah, that sounds about right."

"I went over to the police yard and saw your boat," Claude said. "It was quite a sight. Looked like it had been through Hurricane Katrina."

"We managed to jump clear of the boat before it was hit."

"I've never heard of an alligator as big as twenty feet long, and certainly not twenty-five feet. Did you actually see it?"

"No, it was at night and very dark. We were shinin a spotlight into the water but all we saw was its shadow as it moved through the water beneath the boat. It was a *very* long shadow. That's how we guessed at the size."

"Where were you exactly?"

"South."

"But where, exactly? Southwest or southeast?"

"I don't want to say."

"Would it happen to be somewhere near Gray's Bayou?"

"I don't want to say."

"Why not?"

"I might want to go catch that damn thing. I tell folks where it is and they might go try to do that their self."

"I suppose it might be worth a lot of money; an alligator that big."

"Could be."

"Even photographs."

"Could be."

"How old do you think such an alligator would be? To get that big, I mean."

"I don't know."

"Maybe a hundred years old?"

"Maybe."

"Well, thanks for your time, Mr. LeBlanc."

"No problem."

"You might want to pick up a copy of our next issue. There will be a short article about your experience; and a picture of what's left of your boat."

Claude walked across the street to go see if Mathieu would tell him anything else, but it proved to be a waste of time.

CHAPTER VI

The Hunting

Jizzy bought a single shot .50 calibre rifle in New Orleans two weeks after Labor Day. It took a week to get it after he'd paid his money, since they didn't have them in stock. He didn't bother with a scope. He figured if he ever got to use the rifle that it would be at close quarters in the middle of a swamp, and a scope would actually get in the way. He also bought a .44 magnum pistol for use if the monster got close enough that he felt threatened and he couldn't reload the rifle, and a set of starlight night vision glasses.

He decided that the best and safest way to find the monster was to bait it. He'd read somewhere about a missionary in New Guinea who remarked at a feast about how wonderful the ham he was served tasted, only to find out that it was roasted human flesh. Evidently we taste a lot like pork when we're roasted. So he went to a slaughterhouse and bought a whole fifty-pound pig, cleaned and dressed. If this monster had a taste for human flesh then this was the best he could manage. He put his camping gear in his truck, hitched up his boat and drove to the boat ramp. In another two hours he was back at the site where Alan had met his death.

Tizzy went ashore, armed with his cannon, and searched carefully to be sure that nothing was lurking close by while he put out the bait. He had brought a length of steel cable and he attached a loop to the pig's neck using clamps. He tossed the end over a cypress tree limb and pulled the pig up a few feet off of the ground so that a normal sized gator couldn't reach it. He then anchored the end of the cable to the tree. The monster might eat it off of the cable, but that was the only way this pig was going anywhere. He figured that the carcass might have to hang in the hot sun for a day or two to ripen so that the monster could smell it, and he was prepared to wait.

He went over to the nearest tall cypress with a clear view of the pig and spent the next two hours installing the portable tree stand he used for hunting deer, twenty feet up. He attached a rope and tackle and spent the rest of the afternoon getting his rifle, food, water, high intensity beam flashlight, and mosquito netting up to the stand, and securing them in the branches. It was almost dusk by the time he was finally ready.

Nothing happened that night, the next day or the following night. By the second day he was able to smell the rotting pig and the first turkey vulture appeared. He hadn't planned on that, and since it was a Federal crime to shoot them, he couldn't just start popping them off. He wished that he'd had the good sense to bring a slingshot and a bag of marbles, or even a BB gun; but there was nothing to do about it now.

He watched in frustration as the birds began to slowly but steadily consume the pig, fighting and sparring with each other for a perch on the pig's shoulder. By evening there was little left of the bait, but what there was still had a terrible smell, so he waited, unwilling to leave his perch and go all the way back into Morgan City to buy another pig.

Just after dark he heard the unmistakable sound of something *very* large walking slowly through the muck and water. His heartbeat jumped as adrenaline raced through his body. He put on his night vision glasses and scanned the swamp in the direction of the noise, but couldn't see anything because of the undergrowth, long strands of Spanish moss and tree branches. He decided to focus on the bait.

Whatever was out there was apparently wary. The footsteps had stopped, but after an hour it had not come out from its cover to investigate the ripe bait. "Perhaps it isn't yet hungry," Tizzy thought; "it's only been a few weeks since it ate Alan." He knew that large reptiles like anacondas and crocodilians could go for months between meals.

After another hour Tizzy decided that the creature must have slipped away, and turned off his glasses to get a drink from a plastic bottle. As he was unscrewing the lid he was startled by a loud scream. He dropped the plastic bottle and clicked his night vision glasses back on just in time to see what looked for all the world like an animal straight out of *Jurassic Park* rush out from the brush and snatch away the remains of the pig. It was over in no more than two seconds, and all that was left was the steel cable swinging back and forth. It had been such a fleeting glimpse that Tizzy couldn't even properly describe what he'd seen. All that he could say was that it was reptilian, with a long tail, huge legs and a large head. It obviously had a lot of teeth.

"That goofy billboard with the St. Mary's Parish Boojum isn't that far off," he thought; "though I'm not sure where they got the idea it had feathers. Someone else has seen this thing before, but won't admit to it!"

The monster failed to reappear, and about midday Tizzy descended from his cypress perch with his rifle to go back into town for more bait. He was hopeful that the thing hadn't destroyed his boat, and was relieved to see it intact when he reached it. In another two hours he was back home. His parents had found his note and had begun to get worried. He said hello to his parents and told he was just having fun in the swamp. To their dismay, he informed them that he was going back out. He decided that he wouldn't mention the Boojum. They probably wouldn't believe him anyway, and might well put up a fuss about his return if they did.

He went by the Morgan City mayor's offices and inquired about who had designed the billboard depicting the Boojum west of the city. They referred him to Claude Généroux over at *The Atchafalaya Advocate.*

He went to the newspaper office and found Claude working at his desk, typing away on a PC. He looked up when he walked in.

"*Allo*, Tizzy," he said. "What can I do for you?"

"I'm trying to find out who designed that billboard of the St. Mary's Parish Boojum that's out at the parish line. I was told you might know."

"I do. The sign was based on a description given by an old-timer who said that he'd seen it. He's dead now. The guy who painted it used that as a basis, but embellished it a bit, by puttin feathers on it."

"Why'd he do that?"

"In Lewis Carroll's poem *The Hunting of the Snark* it says that some snarks have feathers and bite. He was just goin along with the poem. Why do you ask?"

"Well, I saw it last night out in the swamp; and it didn't have feathers." Claude's jaw dropped. "You saw it?"

"For only a few seconds, through night vision glasses."

"But how? Where?"

"I baited it with a three day old rotten pig, and climbed into a deer stand I'd mounted in a tree. I was up there for three nights. I meant to shoot it, but it was too fast. I never even managed to get to my rifle up to my shoulder."

"You serious?"

"Yeah; dead serious. It looks just like that picture on that billboard, except without the feathers and wings."

"You were up in a tree with a rifle waiting for it?"

"Yeah; I got me one of them 0.5 calibre rifles, like I told you I was thinkin about doing."

"I don't know whether to believe you or not."

"Don't matter. I saw what I saw. But don't go writin an article about it. You do and I'll come back here some night and burn this place down."

"Are you threatenin me?"

"No; just makin a promise. I don't want anyone out there disturbin that thing until I can get a shot at it."

Claude was silent for a moment. "Let's just say that you actually manage to shoot this thing; will you let me be the first to publish the story?"

"Yeah; no problem."

"Okay. Deal." Tizzy turned to leave. "You be real careful."

"I'm bein so careful you wouldn't believe it. I've seen that thing and I'm not takin any chances." He left and went down to the hardware store and bought a BB gun before going back to the slaughterhouse for another pig.

It took him the rest of the day to string up the new pig and get back into his tree house perch. This time he'd attached the cable to the carcass by wrapping it around it five times so that it wouldn't be so easy to snatch away.

Two days later the first vultures reappeared, but this time he was ready for them. Every time one would land on the bait he would bounce a BB off of its butt. But they were persistent and didn't fly away from nearby trees, too mesmerized by the smell of the rotting pig. Before nightfall there were twenty of them perched in the tops of the trees.

On the third night Tizzy once again heard the monster approach, drawn by the now familiar smell of the bait. Tizzy was ready and focussed his glasses on the pig. This time the Boojum didn't wait so long, and came charging out of the brush after only twenty minutes. When it struck the bait it found it impossible to snatch it away, and whirled to roar in frustration. Tizzy got off one round from his rifle, but it missed, and the Boojum turned to face him, uncannily aware now of where he was.

Before Tizzy could reload the Boojum had crashed through the brush and into the bayou, with an enormous splash. Then all was quiet again. Tizzy scanned the brush along the bank of the bayou, but saw nothing. Then he heard, or rather felt, a strange low frequency noise; it vibrated the tree. A minute later he heard an incredible crash as the Boojum destroyed his boat. At first Tizzy couldn't figure out what had happened, but it slowly dawned on him.

Over the next several nights the Boojum would make fleeting appearances, too quick for Tizzy to get off a shot with the huge rifle which was designed for sniping at long distance, not for a shootout. He was too terrified to descend from the tree, knowing that the Boojum was waiting for just that. He had calculated that his limited provisions would last for only another five days, even if he rationed them carefully. He could manage to get water by coming down the tree just long enough to fill a bottle with the greenish swamp water that surrounded the tree, but he knew that if he was stuck in the tree for weeks he would likely starve.

On three occasions he tried to bait the Boojum with himself, to get off a shot, but the huge rifle was much too unwieldy for an animal as quick as this one. By the time he would get it up to his shoulder it would have disappeared once again. He finally gave up on the rifle, even though he realized that it was probably the only thing he had with enough force to kill it. He tried the same tactics with his pistol. But that wasn't much better. He got several opportunities to shoot, but found that his aim was too bad with the pistol. Finally down to one remaining bullet he decided to save it for himself, if worse came to worst.

A game warden found him two weeks later during a huge manhunt that was organized after the pleading of Claude Généroux and Tizzy's family. He had put a bullet through his chest, still perched up in the tree. Heavy rain had long since obliterated the Boojum's tracks, and it was a matter of wide debate and discussion about why Tizzy had killed himself up in a tree. Claude didn't tell them that he knew why he was up there. He didn't want to be responsible for anyone else trying to hunt down the Boojum. Somehow he felt responsible for what had happened, since he hadn't tried harder to stop him, or advised the Sheriff what he was up to. Perhaps they could have rescued him had they known his approximate location.

The biggest mistake Tizzy made was not taking along a cell phone. He could have used some F-4s for close ground support.

CHAPTER VII

The Boots

Dave Thibodeau took his bass boat out on Big Wax Bayou for some night fishing. He had lived in the Morgan City area all of his life and worked offshore on drilling platforms and on salt marsh oil rigs. He needed fresh air and wide-open spaces to recover from the stifling close living quarters and the sulphur-laden air on the platform. He loved the outdoors and went hunting and fishing whenever he could.

He had been divorced for eight years and didn't really miss anything about Terra except her fine Cajun cooking, which, unfortunately, had clogged his arteries. His two girls were grown and married, one of them living over in the New Orleans suburb of Kenner, where she and her husband owned a little hole-in-the-wall Cajun restaurant, and the other over in Lake Charles, where she worked as a cocktail waitress in a casino. So he had nothing to keep him at home. He spent most of his money on gambling, drinking, cold-hearted women, boats, guns, and fishing trips.

He had just caught a little three-pound bass and was taking the hook out of its mouth when the Boojum came straight up out of the water right behind the fish, so fast that Dave didn't even have time to jump back out of the way. All he saw was a huge gaping mouth lined with rows of six-inch long serrated teeth. He tried to scream, but the Boojum ate the sound when its jaws closed over his head. When the Boojum sank back into the bayou Dave went with it. He had vanished suddenly enough, though not quietly, and certainly without any glee. The bass escaped to tell the tale to his fishy buddies.

About fifteen minutes later Dave's right foot, still in his boot and bitten off at the ankle, floated up from the bottom of the bayou and washed up against the bank. It would eventually float down the bayou, out into Sweet Bay Lake, and then on out into the Gulf, where it would finally be netted by a shrimper, ten days after a game warden found his expensive boat tied up along the bank of Big Wax Bayou.

DNA analysis of the foot would later confirm that it had belonged to Dave Thibodeau. Out of fear of getting AIDS from tainted blood, he had donated some of his own blood for an upcoming coronary bypass; so the police were able to say with certainty that the foot had indeed once belonged to him. Because of the circumstances of his terrible demise the paper referred to him as "The Boots", a name that would stick in the chronicles of the local Boojum legend.

There wasn't really enough left of him to justify a coffin, but his daughters wanted a proper funeral, with something to bury. So the undertaker put Dave's foot and boot in a child's coffin, along with some fishing lures that the girls dropped by the mortuary before they sealed the coffin. They wanted him to have something to catch flying fish with on the other side of the rainbow.

Terra came to the funeral, dressed in black from her hat to her shoes, but really wasn't at all sad to see Dave go. The priest tried to assure her and the girls that, being a Catholic, he'd gone to heaven to be with Jesus, the Blessed Virgin, and the angels. Terra knew better; if there was room in Heaven for someone as mean as Dave Thibodeau had been in life, then Hell would surely prove to be an almost empty place.

Blue Boojum

Blue Boojum

Rufus Broussard held a small sign with "Oran Lafleur" handwritten on it against his chest, standing patiently in the Hobby Airport in Houston waiting for arriving passengers from a Southwest Airlines flight from San Diego. It wasn't long until a tall young man, dressed in West Texas cowboy-style clothes and wearing worn snakeskin boots, walked up to him and said, "You must be my ride. I'm Oran." He stuck out his hand and smiled.

Rufus lowered the sign and shook his hand. "That's me, a.k.a., Blue Boojum Taxi Service." He laughed softly. "I'm Rufus Broussard. It's nice to meet you, Oran."

Ten minutes later they were in the airport parking structure where Rufus had parked his Blue Boojum Environmental Services extended-cab four-wheel drive pick-up, which was naturally painted a bright metallic blue.

"How long have you been with Blue Boojum?" Rufus asked once they were on the Gulf Freeway heading north to get onto I-10 to Lake Charles.

"Since I graduated from A&M three years ago. Class of '08."

"I'm surprised we haven't come across each other before."

"Yeah, it's odd. I've heard your name often enough, of course. I've been working in California ever since the big San Diego quake. How many years do you think it'll be before the Feds allow people to move back into southern Louisiana and Mississippi?"

"I'd guess twenty years, at least, but personally I wouldn't ever move back in, especially if I had kids or a young wife. That bomb was very dirty. There's some bad stuff that's going to linger for centuries."

Oran nodded. "Yeah. It's one thing to get suited up and go in for a few hours, and quite another to move back in to live. Perhaps we could give it all back to the French."

Rufus laughed. "That's a good idea! We could even give them a fifteen-million dollar refund to sweeten the deal. You should write the State Department and suggest it."

"I think I'll do that, but I'm sure the French wouldn't take it back even if we offered them fifteen billion. It's a real shame what those sons of bitches did. America'll never be the same."

Rufus nodded. "It's the true price of Saudi oil. It's what happens when you deal with the Devil."

A few hours later they drove into Lake Charles and pulled into the small parking lot outside the controlled access barrier that had been erected across the Interstate. Rufus waved at the MPs stationed at the barrier gate as they went into the office. The MPs saluted back, as if they were officers. They walked up to the desk to sign in.

"Well, if it ain't a Boojum!" the smiling woman behind the counter said by way of greeting Rufus.

Rufus nodded and grinned broadly. "Two of em, actually! How ya doin, Louise?"

"Doin just great, Rufus!" she replied. "Who's your friend?"

"Louise, this is Oran," he said. "Oran Lafleur. He also works for Blue Boojum. He'll be going into the hot zone with me today to learn the routine and help collect some samples."

"Nice to meet you, Louise," Oran said as he handed her his Blue Boojum ID. She frowned. "You guys ought to stay out of there, you know."

Rufus nodded. "Yeah, I know. I only go in there when I have to. Every three months is plenty often enough."

"You guys are brave," she said. "They'd never get me in there."

"Naw, we ain't brave, we're just typical contractors. We'll just do dang near anything legal as long as the money is right," Rufus said.

"I don't believe that! You're listed under 'B' for 'Brave' in my Rolodex."

They signed in on the computer and then Louise handed them their passes and radiation badges. "Mr. Lafleur, you're required to stay with Rufus at all times, since it's your first time going in there. It's for your own safety, not that we don't trust you. Don't pick up and take out anything except your samples. It might pose a serious health risk to others."

Oran nodded. "I understand. No problem. There's nothing in there that I want. I could see a thousand dollar bill on the pavement and step right over it."

They drove east on abandoned I-10 for about twelve miles to the Alexandria exit, then headed northeast. "You ever been to Ground Zero?" Rufus asked.

"No, this is my first time. I'm curious of course, but I'd been hoping that I'd never have to go in there. I've seen pictures, of course."

"It's not too dangerous to approach it from the west. As you know, the prevailing winds at the time of the blast carried almost all of the fallout south and southeast. Baton Rouge, Morgan City, and New Orleans really got nailed. It wasn't fair. They'd just started getting rebuilt a little after Katrina and then they all had to pack up and leave again. In my opinion, New Orleans won't ever be repopulated now. It's toast."

"When do we need to suit up?"

"Not till we get within about ten miles of the red zone. There's a checkpoint and decontamination facility at a little berg named Lecompte. Once we're suited up we'll head east on the parish road over to where Moreauville used to be, where we'll switch into an all-terrain vehicle that the Government keeps there for people heading into the Zone."

"What happened to Moreauville?"

"It got fried. There's nothing there now except for a special Government admin. building for people like us comin and goin. It's pressurized with elaborate filtration, lead shielding in the walls, decontamination facilities, disposable clothing, etc."

"How far from there to the crater?"

"Ten miles, give or take."

"Is there a decent road into the zone?"

"I wouldn't dignify it by callin it a road. It's just a rough cleared track, really. But that's not a problem. The Government's swamp buggy is amphibious, with huge tires, so it can easily get us there, right across the old rice fields and ponds if necessary, though we'll try to stay on the track. We wouldn't make it a hundred yards through the mud in this truck."

It took a little more than an hour to get to what was left of Alexandria.

"It's just a ghost town now," Rufus said as they approached the outskirts. "It's illegal to even enter without a special Federal permit. It was far enough away from the blast zone that there wasn't a lot of blast and fire damage, but it's still hot from radiation. The Air Force flew over a month after the blast and used smart bombs to flatten most of the buildings to discourage people from trying to move back in. The only things moving in town now are a few mutant cats and possums, and the security cameras that continuously scan the empty streets looking for intruders."

"People actually try to come back?"

"Some do. Home's home, I guess, and some folks don't want to leave it, no matter what. It's amazing how thick-headed some people can be. If the cameras pick them up the Army sends in a rescue team in moon suits and arrests them. If they resist too hard the Team is authorized to use deadly force. They have a zero-tolerance order and they enforce it so people understand that it's deadly serious, but they haven't had to shoot anyone yet, thank goodness. They fine them fifteen thousand dollars the first time they catch them, to pay for the search and rescue costs. If they come back in again they lock them up at taxpayer expense for six months in a Federal prison over in East Texas, in addition to a repeat fine for costs."

"And the third time?"

"That'll get them a mandatory fifty-thousand-dollar fine and five years in jail. There haven't been any three-time losers that I've heard of. But to tell the truth, I wouldn't be surprised to learn that someone's been living in there in some basement. Louisiana has its fair share of crazies."

About a mile outside of Alexandria the highway made a wide loop, heading southeast towards Lecompte.

"I see they've put up a barrier across the highway," Oran remarked, looking back at what remained of Alexandria.

"Yeah. All highways and roads into Alexandria have been cut with deep trenches and blocked by concrete barriers. They resemble tank traps. They've erected a high chain-link fence with razor wire all the way around the town. It's amazing what they have to do to protect people from themselves."

Once they arrived in Lecompte they suited up and were driven into Moreauville in a big white Suburban by an MP, also dressed in protective gear. They drove up to a metal clad building that housed the swamp buggy and the MP pushed a garage door opener that raised a roll-up door to let them inside. "I'll return for you at 1600 hours sharp," the MP told them. "Please be here on time. If you are not here by 1700 hours a search team will be sent in for you, but that won't make people happy. The buggy has a GPS tracking device, so stay with it. In case you get into trouble it will make it easy to locate you. Look out for snakes."

"We'll be here on time," Rufus assured him as he and Oran got out. They stashed the cases of equipment they would use for sampling and drove out.

The MP re-closed the garage door and saluted as they drove by.

Al-Qaeda in America had smuggled the bomb into the States across the porous Mexican/Arizona border before the concrete border fence had finally been erected by Homeland Security to stop illegal immigration. Mexico was furious about the wall, and had even threatened to go to war over it, though they hadn't seriously considered it, of course. The most immediate result of the fence had been a quantum leap in the street price for narcotics and a rise in crime to pay for it.

The bomb was a sophisticated "suitcase" device, manufactured in the old Soviet Union during the last days of the Cold War. It had been stolen and smuggled into Iran by six disgruntled Russian soldiers, who hadn't been paid in months.

They received the equivalent of USD 10,000 in what turned out to be Iranian-counterfeited notes. They had been promptly arrested by Russian authorities shortly after trying to exchange one of the large notes in a bank in Kyzylorda, Kazakhstan. They had been taken to a secret military prison in order to cover up the politically sensitive loss of a portable thermonuclear device.

The bomb was packed in a large aluminum suitcase that was typically used for expensive camera gear. It weighed almost 250 pounds, requiring either two strong men or one weightlifter to handle it. It had left Iran aboard an Iranian submarine to a location in international waters off of the west coast of Baja California, where it had been picked up at night by a fishing boat out of Los Mochis, where there was an Al-Qaeda sleeper cell, whose members would undertake the task of smuggling it into the United States.

They were intercepted by two US Border Patrol officers three miles inside the Sonoran Desert south of Tucson, but the well-armed terrorists had quickly overpowered them. Their bullet-riddled bodies had been dumped at the base of an endangered thirty-foot tall boojum tree and covered with stones. Their remains would be discovered three days later by a graduate student from the University of Arizona who was studying this exquisite specimen for his thesis.

From there the bomb had been transported across the vast emptiness of southern Arizona, New Mexico, and West Texas, before finally crossing into Louisiana near Shreveport on a very early Sunday morning when the weigh station at the Texas-Louisiana border was closed. It was placed in a high-security, air-conditioned self-storage unit in a cabinet lined with thick lead shielding as a precaution against detection by Homeland Security agents, who occasionally monitored self-storage facilities for trace radiation levels. The bomb would remain undetected in cold storage until the upcoming Fourth of July holiday.

Rufus drove the buggy. "We won't go all the way in. There's a place about a mile upriver from the crater where you can get a pretty good view of what happened. We can collect samples there as well."

Thirty minutes later they pulled onto an old elevated conservancy road atop the levee on the west bank of the Red River and drove south a few miles before stopping. Rufus got out, signaling to Oran that he should join him. They walked over to the edge of the riverbank.

"You can see where the Red River now joins the Mississippi," he said, pointing in that direction. "The old Mississippi channel went that way, to the southeast, towards Baton Rouge and New Orleans. It's pretty much dried up now. There are some pools the size of small lakes in the old riverbed, of course, but normal flow is gone.

"When the bomb went off it tore out a huge section of the west bank, releasing the Mississippi to flow southwest, where it naturally wanted to go, no longer restrained by the levees. The Red River channel wasn't nearly big enough to handle the massive new flow, so the merged rivers spread out along the way. There are sections now that are more than a mile wide. It'll be a while before it cuts a deeper channel. The river's no longer navigable by commercial shipping, of course. Perhaps some day when the radiation subsides they'll dredge a new channel and try to restore the waterway.

"The Red River was less than a mile away from where the Mississippi burst out. The sudden flow caused massive flooding all along the river. It swallowed up what used to be the Atchafalaya as it went, sweeping away the towns of

Simmesport, Melville, and Krotz Springs, before dumping into Grand Lake. It then devastated Morgan City before finally flowing into Atchafalaya Bay and the Gulf."

"How many people died in the attack?" Oran asked.

"Nobody knows for sure. The detonation was in a rural area, so the blast and fireball probably didn't kill all that many outright. But thousands died in the massive flooding, for which there had been no warning, and lots more have since died of radiation poisoning and cancer. As you know, it was an intentionally dirty bomb."

On the 4th of July 2009, at 5:30 a.m., an old Chrysler mini-van with Louisiana plates turned south at Vidalia onto the conservancy road that ran along the top of the levee on the Mississippi riverbank. The burly Arab driver got out, cut the chain on the access gate and drove through. He re-closed the gate so that it didn't look like anyone had gone through, but opening the gate had triggered an alarm back in Vidalia. However, it would be fifteen minutes before the police would dispatch a patrolman to investigate. Approximately twenty-seven miles downriver, near a point where the Mississippi was less than five miles from the Red River, the driver stopped the mini-van and got out, taking a prayer rug he had brought with him. He walked about fifty feet up the road and spread the rug out onto the ground, then returned to the back of the van, where he opened the door to access an aluminum suitcase. With considerable effort he lugged the small but very heavy suitcase down the embankment of the levee and placed it against the stone-faced wall at the base of the levee to direct the blast. He undid the clasps and opened the hinged lid, exposing the sophisticated thermonuclear device that was one of the high points of Soviet nuclear technical achievement. Inside the case, next to the device, was a pamphlet, printed in Cyrillic, which he couldn't read. Assuming that it was simply instructions for arming and triggering the device he had tossed it into the weeds. In fact, the pamphlet was a rare Uzbek-Russian bilingual translation of *The Hunting of the Snark* that had been placed there as a joke by Vladimir Ivanovich, one of the Russian soldiers involved in the original theft. Vladimir had met his own personal boojum two days following his arrest and interrogation when an Internal Security officer had placed a pistol against the base of his skull and executed him in the prison basement.

Repeating a memorized twenty-step sequence, the driver armed the bomb, setting the digital timer for two-minutes. He closed the suitcase lid, as if it mattered, and then scrambled back up to the road and his prayer rug. Glancing at a small compass he had brought with him, he checked to be sure he was aligned with Mecca and commenced saying his final prayers, hoping for Heaven and a bevy of beautiful virgins with whom to spend eternity as a reward for his glorious martyrdom. Thirty-seconds later a Louisiana State Police patrol car came roaring up behind the mini-van in a cloud of dust, siren blaring. The trooper got out, unholstered his pistol and walked up to the man who had his forehead pressed to the carpet, mumbling something in Arabic.

"What do you think you're d—"

Before he could finish his question the bomb detonated with the explosive force of ten megatons, instantly vaporizing the old mini-van, the hopeful terrorist, the angry trooper and his patrol car, and the rare *Snark* edition, and simultaneously creating an enormous crater where the reinforced bank that had long kept Old Man River in his historic channel.

The force of the blast vaporized the water in a half-mile section of the river and actually backed up the flow. Then, regaining its flow, it had surged through the breech, an unstoppable wall of muddy radioactive water heading for the Red River.

Rufus and Oran spent the afternoon collecting water and soil samples up and down the conservancy road. Having completed their task they turned around and headed back for Moreauville.

When they drove up to the building they found that the SUV that had come to pick them up had been completely wrecked.

Rufus parked next it and they both clambered out to investigate what might have happened. They found the roof peeled back like the lid on a can of beans crudely opened with a hunting knife. The driver was gone and there was lots of blood.

Looking at the ground they quickly noticed dozens of impressions of very large footprints that resembled the tracks one might see in a dinosaur museum. The animal that had made them had circled the SUV several times. Rufus and Oran were both in shock, uncertain what to do.

"What the heck made these prints?" Oran said, bending down to examine the nearly three-foot long impressions more closely. "Have you ever seen anything like this?"

"No, and I don't believe in dragons or Jabberwocks," Rufus said. "The only thing I can imagine is some sort of monster alligator."

Oran laughed nervously. "Yeah, right! A fifty-foot gator!"

"I'm open to suggestions."

“I have no idea, but I don’t believe in live dinosaurs either; this ain’t Jurassic Park!”

“Where’s the driver’s body?” Rufus said, standing back up and scanning the horizon. “Look! There’s a trail of blood leading that way.” He was pointing to the left of the metal building in which the buggy was normally stored.

They followed the trail for a closer look. “He was bleeding out fast,” Oran observed.

“Look there,” Rufus remarked, fear easily detectable in his voice, pointing a little ways over towards a grisly object on the grass.

“What is it?” Oran asked, almost afraid to ask.

Rufus walked over to examine it closely. “It’s a man’s left hand. Something’s severed it from the arm just above the wrist. It’s still got a wedding ring on! It’s likely what’s left of our driver. Look, I’ve seen enough. Let’s get back in the buggy and head for Lecompte. I’ll drive while you contact the military. Here’s my cell phone. We aren’t armed and we could be in big trouble if whatever this thing is decides to attack us as well.”

“You don’t have to convince me!” Oran assured him, turning back and jogging towards the buggy.

Oran phoned in and briefly explained what they had found. Before they reached Lecompte they saw a pair of Blackhawk helicopters on their way towards Moreauville.

It took the better part of an hour to get Rufus and Oran decontaminated and debriefed. Naturally, at first everyone had been skeptical of their preposterous story, and there had been some joking about Godzilla. However, when the first reports from the search teams confirmed their account the laughter had stopped and everyone turned deadly serious.

Eventually, US Army Captain Ian M. Baker came into the debriefing room and sat down at the table in front of Rufus and Oran. "This entire incident has been declared Top Secret. That means you are both now expressly forbidden, for the rest of your lives, to talk to anyone other than a properly identified Federal Agent about anything you have seen or experienced today. Failure to comply with this strict order will result in your immediate incarceration in an undisclosed military facility. Your chances of ever being released or heard from again are basically nil. Do you understand?"

"You can't do that," Rufus protested. "We have rights, including the right of *habeas corpus* and against false imprisonment."

"I can tell that you're going to be a problem, Mr. Broussard. I'm not even going to mess with you." Captain Baker stood up and walked out of the room, returning a few moments later with two MPs, who placed Rufus in handcuffs behind his back. "You are under arrest, Mr. Broussard," Captain Baker informed him.

"You can't do this!" Rufus protested loudly. "I haven't done anything! I demand to speak to my attorney." Captain Baker ignored him while the MPs drug him out, kicking and screaming.

Once things were quiet again the Captain turned back to Oran. "You seem like a more reasonable person, Mr. Lafleur. If you agree to cooperate you will be flown to a high security Federal facility in an undisclosed location in the South Pacific, where you will spend the next several months cooling your heels. It's a nice place: swimming; golf; exotic food. If it can be determined that you can keep your mouth shut you may eventually be released, under very strict conditions. Do you think you can do that, or do you want to speak to your attorney?"

Oran thought about it for a few seconds before making the obvious decision. "I enjoy golf and I like to eat. I'd also like to work on my tan."

"Good." Captain Baker went back out of the room and returned with another MP. "You need to go with this man, Mr. Lafleur. You should resist any urge to make trouble for him. He is very well trained and carries papers authorizing him to use lethal force to control you should that be necessary. Do exactly whatever he instructs you to do. Don't try to start up conversations with him. For your own safety, don't start a fight with him; believe me, you don't want to mess with him. You will end up dead. Can you do that, Mr. Lafleur?"

"Absolutely," Oran assured him.

"Good. You have a nice vacation, Sir."

Upon arrival at the Moreauville site the Army deployed several platoons to track whatever it was that had attacked the MP, having brought several bloodhounds with them. They secured the area, and since night was fast approaching, conducted their search using night vision and infrared goggles. The dogs easily followed the creature and the blood trail, which went straight for the widely flooded area where the Mississippi and Red Rivers had merged, the tracks going straight into the river. They radioed back for their choppers and spent the next five hours slowly flying along the river banks using powerful searchlights and infrared scanners to search the banks, but found nothing but ordinary wildlife. They finally returned to Lecompte empty-handed.

A forensics team back at Moreauville collected the severed hand and numerous blood samples for DNA testing to confirm the identity of whom they thought had been killed, and made plaster casts of all of the bizarre footprints, which would be used in an attempt by zoologists and paleontologists to try to identify the creature and estimate its weight. None of them bought the idea that it was a giant gator.

Three months later, two members of a military patrol investigating reports of illegal poaching activity in the still-radioactive swamps outside of what had once been Morgan City, abruptly disappeared. Search and rescue teams were quickly flown in and eventually discovered what remained of their air-boat, along with traces of blood on the vegetation around the site, but no bodies. Forensics experts were flown in and treated the site as a crime scene, collecting blood samples for DNA analysis and making plaster casts of a few very large footprints that resembled those a large dinosaur.

Similarities between this incident and the earlier incident at Moreauville were quickly recognized by The Pentagon. DNA analysis identified the two missing soldiers, but other blood samples were puzzling. The lab report said that the blood was from an unidentified species.

In spite of The Pentagon's best efforts to keep a lid on everything that had happened near Morgan City, rumors were soon cropping up about the return of what had once been referred to in coastal Louisiana newspapers as the "Atchafalaya Boojum". The *National Enquirer* devoted an entire issue to resurrecting the old legends and stories that had become the staple of the South Louisiana monster legend, though the *Enquirer* as yet knew nothing about the recent disappearance of Rufus and Oran's military chauffeur.

Rufus Broussard had spent the time since his arrest in a secret CIA prison embedded in a mine shaft that had been used in the 1950s to store nuclear weapons in the Manzano

Mountains north of Albuquerque. After screaming his head off for several weeks he had finally decided that this was pointless and had settled into watching a great deal of TV. Oran Lafleur had spent the same time in a Quonset hut on Johnston Atoll, south of the Hawaiian Islands. The Captain's promise of golf, swimming, and exotic food had been somewhat exaggerated. Oran was getting pretty tired of fried Spam and Coca-Cola, and putting a single golf ball around on the green carpet in his living quarters into a drinking glass. He did, however, have a gorgeous tan.

Within a few weeks of the latest disappearances at Morgan City wild rumors appeared about a mutant-Boojum that had been created by radioactive fallout. What people didn't understand was that the creature was nothing new, but had only recently made itself more visible because it had been forced to wander out of its normal hunting range in the swamps in search of something to eat, due to the forced evacuation of normal human populations and the massive kills of alligators and nutria that had been its staple diet, due to radiation poisoning.

Three years after 7/04 the CIA finally confirmed rumors that the bomb used to divert the course of the Mississippi had been transported across the Pacific in an Iranian submarine purchased from France with oil exports. Reacting to Iran's complicity and fearing that the next suitcase bomb they sent over would be detonated in the heart of a major American city, newly-elected President sent a blunt warning to the Iranian government through the Egyptian Ambassador to the United States, demanding the immediate dismantling of all of their nuclear facilities or face a unilateral American preemptive nuclear strike "that will do the job for you."

When it became obvious that Iran had no intention of doing any such thing she recalled the American ambassadors and embassy staffs in all countries with significant Muslim populations, closed those embassies, and placed the military on high alert. Over the next two months all American forces were withdrawn from military bases in Europe and the Middle East. These actions immediately resulted in all-out civil war in Iraq and sent the world into virtual hysterics, condemning the United States for nuclear brinkmanship and provocation.

However, few governments seriously believed that the United States would actually do such an unthinkable and irresponsible thing as to nuke Iran, reminding themselves that the United States had reassured the world for decades that it would not use nuclear weapons as a first-strike option. However, as a precaution, France and Russia wisely pulled out their own personnel who were clandestinely assisting the Iranians in their uranium enrichment efforts. Two weeks after America had pulled back into her defensive posture, the President reissued her demand a third time. When it was again obvious that Iran had no intention of complying, she ordered the strike without consulting Congress. The attack included newly developed deep-penetration, bunker-busting nuclear warheads, launched from submarines. Eighty percent of the primary nuclear processing and manufacturing facilities across Iran were either destroyed or severely damaged, along with substantial collateral loss of life, including many of Iran's top nuclear technologists and scientists.

In sharp contrast to the lukewarm condemnation expressed by almost every government about the Louisiana nuclear terrorist strike, there had been great shock and rabid, near-universal condemnation of the American response against Iran, even from its closest allies, with the single exception of

Israel. When most countries broke off diplomatic and commercial relations with the United States and withdrew their ambassadors, Congress responded by withdrawing American membership in the United Nations, removed its lop-sided financial support, closed UN headquarters, and gave all UN staff 48 hours to leave or be arrested and expelled. The whole pack gradually relocated to Bonn, occupying some of the huge governmental office buildings that had been vacated when the German capital had been relocated to Berlin.

The Iranian President had naturally gone ballistic after the attack and had predictably responded by firing a nuclear-tipped cruise missile at Jerusalem. Anticipating that this might happen, Israel was on high alert and waiting. The missile was intercepted and destroyed over the Arabian Desert by one of three Israeli-modified Patriot missiles that were fired at it. A week later, Israel retaliated by dropping a low-yield neutron bomb on Tehran, with consequent casualties approaching a hundred thousand. As Fate would have it, the President had been one of these casualties, having been practically struck on the head by the incoming warhead while participating in an anti-American street demonstration, fulfilling, in the minds of a great many Americans, his shouted admonition for “death to the Great Satan”.

Somehow forgetting that it had been Iran’s intention to destroy Jerusalem and all of its inhabitants, most governments had joined the Muslim world in calling for the immediate destruction of Israel. However, they had all been too intimidated by obvious Israeli nuclear superiority to actually do anything except rant and rail against them. A great many American and Israeli flags were burned.

Fearing that the world was steadily descending into a global nuclear holocaust, the EU quickly negotiated a rather one-sided mutual-defense pact with Israel in order to stabilize the Middle East, giving Russia pause to reconsider the wisdom of its initial intention of "doing the Muslim world a favor" by destroying the Jewish state, something that would have inevitably brought a massive nuclear retaliation by Israel's only genuine earthly ally.

The net result of these unprecedented events had been the total collapse of the world's economy and the onset of a deep, world-wide economic depression. Lacking the resources to combat it, over a third of the world's population died within the coming year from a combination of a pandemic of several newly emergent viruses and starvation. America was not exempt, losing a third of its own population as well, along with its super-power and world leader status.

The American President was eventually impeached for initiating the Iranian nuclear strike without Congressional approval. Vice-President Charles "Bubba" Schlarg, the former Senator from North Carolina, was sworn in as President.

For Congress had decided that Schlarg was a Boojum, you see.

Southern Fried Snark

Southern Fried Snark

Bubba eased himself onto the porch swing next to Alice. The moon was full and the humid night air was sweet with the fragrance of Confederate Jasmine. You could hear the comforting dull-roar of big rigs on the distant Interstate and the sounds of the neighbor's teenage kids wrestling in their bedroom with the windows open.

"Mind iffen I sit with you here in the moonlight fer a spell, Alice?"

"I reckon I don't mind," she said and then took a sip of her RC. "What you been up to, Bubba?"

"I was jest listnin te NPR on the radio. They was a-playin this old record of a Lewis Carroll poem, read by that ole movie actor that played Frankenstein—Boris Karloff."

"You mean the same Lewis Carroll what wrote *Alice in Wonderland*?"

"Yeah. That's him!"

"Momma named me after his Alice. D'you know that?"

"I sort o figgered as much. Karloff wasn't readin *Alice* though. He was a-readin *The Huntin o the Snark*. You ever heared o that one?"

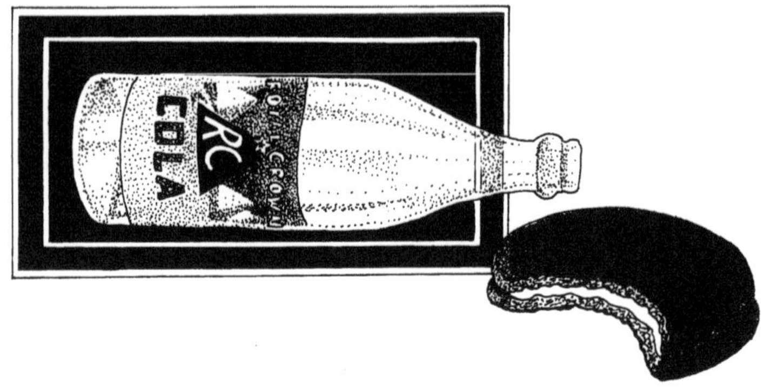

"No, I don't reckon I have. You want a drink o ma RC?" She held the bottle towards Bubba and smiled sweetly.

"Thank you kinely, Alice. Don't mind if I do." He took a big swig then handed the bottle back to her. "I jest love RC Cola! Specially with a Milky Way bar."

"Me too! They's both some o ma favorites. You know, Bubba, I never would'a guessed you was a NPR listner an was partial te poetry."

"I ain't, normally. But this here poem was funny an I jest kept on a-listnin in spite o masef. It was so funny that I think I can remember most of it."

"What's a 'snark', anyways?" she asked. "I don't think I ever seen a pitchure o one."

"I still ain't quite sure—even after a-hearin the poem. I do know that it's a mysterious and dangerous beast."

"Sort of like a cornered possum?" she asked.

"No, more like a razorback, I reckon. Reeeally dangerous!"

"You corner a possum an it can be dangerous as all git out! I seen one bite the nose off a dawg once't! Poor thang bled like a stuck hog. They had to take it to the vet an git stitches. That dawg never could hunt agin, what with his nose all stitched up and everthang. Could'n smell nothin!"

"You're right! A cornered possum's real mean—when he ain't playin daid, o course. But the Snark is meaner yet! Specially one kind of em, callt a 'Boojum'."

"You talking bout that monster what's sposed to live over in the swamps round Morgan City?"

"Could be. I ain't sure. Same name, though."

"Can you repeat some of the poem fer me?"

"I dunno, Alice; you jest might git skeered."

"Naw. I'll be fine. I like skeery movies. I ain't never been skeered of a poem afore."

"Like which movie, fer instance?"

"Wall, one o ma favorites is *Nightmare on Wonderland Avnue*."

Bubba nodded. "Yeah! That one's skeery all right! A chain saw in the hands of a crazy person wearin a Mad Hatter's hat makes me right narvish. Wall, I cain't member the rhymin in the poem, but I think I could tell you the jist of it, iffen you'd like to hear some of it."

"I'd like that right much, Bubba. It don't matter iffen you rhyme it or not. How's it go?"

"Wall, it starts somethin like this:

"I reckon this here's jest the place fer a Snark!" the
Bellman hollered,
As he carried his crew to the shore…"

"Scuse me, Bubba, can I ast you somethin?"

"Sure, Alice."

"What's a bellman?"

"Best I unnerstan it, he's the captain of a ship an he rings his bell to signal his crew te do thangs. Sort o like blowin a whistle at a huntin dawg."

"Why'd he have te carry em?"

"I reckon maybe they could'n swim."

"Now that's right curious. Sailors what cain't swim! You wouldn't git me out on the Guf in a boat iffen I could'n swim! No way!"

"Yep. I agree wit'ya. Like I said, it's a funny poem. Shall I go on ahead with it?"

"Yes, please. I'm sorry I interrupted you."

"Naw, that's all right. You jest interrupt me anytime you want to. I don't mind. Anyways—

He was a-holdin each one of em up on top o the surf
By one of his fangers tangled up in their hair."

"Ouch!" Alice exclaimed.

"You jest git bit by a skeeter?" Bubba asked.

"No, I was jest thinkin bout gittin carried somewhar by ma hair! That'd hurt!"

"I reckon," Bubba said while nodding, then continued:

"This here's jest the place fer a Snark!" the Bellman hollers agin,
"That ought te encourage ma crew.
Jest the place fer a Snark! Thar! I done said it three times!
What I tell you three times is a pure an simple fact!"

"Would'n it be nice iffen it was that simple?" Alice asked. "Jest sayin somethin three times makin it true?"

"Fer sure! Why, I could say 'I got me a new truck! I got me a new truck! I got me a new truck!' An there'd be this purty red Chevy a-sittin out in the front yard fer me!"

"Whoo-ee! That would be nice, fer sure! Keep on a-goin," she encouraged him.

"He had a big crew an one of em was a boot..."

"A boot?" Alice said, laughing. "Did you say a boot?"

"That's what he said. I don't rightly know what a 'boot' is."

"Bubba, don't you know nothin? A boot's what you put on yer foot!"

Bubba laughed. "Shoot, Alice! I know that! But I don't think that's what he meant. Mebbe he was a soldier AWOL out o bootcamp."

"Mebbe. This poem sure nuff *is* funny!" Alice said, giggling. "Go on!" She poked him lightly in the ribs and Bubba laughed.

"An another one of em was some guy that makes
Bonnets an Hats."

"What kind o bonnets an hats?" Alice wanted to know. "You mean fer girls?"

"Beats the heck out o me! But, I'm a-thinkin probly huntin caps an camo rain gear. After all, they's on a huntin trip!"

This seemed to make sense to Alice, who nodded and took another sip of RC, while fluttering her hand like a Luna Moth to indicate that Bubba should continue.

"He also brung along a Bartender to keep em from
fittin,
An a Stock Broker to invest their money.

This also seemed to make sense to Alice, who let him continue uninterrupted.

Thar was also a Pool Shark on board, whose skill was
mazin,
An he probly would'a took all their money
Cept fer the fact that the Bellman brung along this
Banker
To lock up all o their cash fer em…

And there was also a Beaver...”

“A beaver?” Alice interrupted. “You mean a *woman?*”

“No, I don’t think so. I’m purty sure that this here Beaver is the kind with big teeth an a flat tail.”

“Shoot, Bubba! That sounds like half the girls I know!”

Bubba laughed. “What I’m tryin te describe fer you, Alice, is one o them big brown rodents that lives in a pond!”

“Shoot, Bubba! Them ain’t beavers! They’s nutria!”

“Nutria don’t got flat tails!”

“They do iffen they gits it runned over on the highway!” Alice laughed.

“You got to quit pullin ma leg iffen you want te hear the rest of this poem!”

“Okay, okay, sorry. I’ll let up. I jest thought it was funny te think about this bunch o guys on a boat goin on a huntin trip with a pet beaver.”

“You’re right. It *is* funny. The whole blame poem’s funnier than yer Granny in a two-piece bathin suit.”

Alice laughed just thinking about that and took another sip of RC. “I sure wisht I had a Milky Way! Then things’d be jest bout perfeck!”

“I’ll go git you one at the 7-11 when I’m through tellin you this here poem. Like I was sayin:

There was also a Beaver that would walk on the deck,
Or else sit up in the bow makin lace.”

“Lace?” Alice demanded. “The beaver made lace?”

“That’s what I heared. Lace.”

“That settles it! That beaver’s a woman! I don’t care what you say!”

Bubba smiled and shrugged. “Okay. Think what you want. Shall I go on?”

"Sorry! Yes, yes. Git a-goin!"

"The Bellman kept tellin em that the Beaver had often saved em from sinkin,
But he didn't esplain exackly how.

There was also this fella that was famous cause of all the thangs
He plumb fergot when he got onto the boat.
Like his tree-stan, an his sleepin bag, an his tent.
And that's not all! He fergot all of the rest o his gear as well."

"He sounds like a idjit, iffen you ast me!" Alice remarked. "He probly even fergot his gun!"

"I think you're right. I didn't hear nothin in the rest o the poem about no rifle."

"I knew it. A total idjit! It'd serve him right iffen that Snark was te et him! Is that what happens? Does he git et?"

"I ain't sayin 'yes' or 'no'! That'd ruin the surprise endin! Anyway,

"He brung forty-two boxes of carefully packed gear,
With his name wrote on each one of em,
But he fergot te mention this te the Captain,
So they sailed off with em all still a-sittin on the dock!"

Alice laughed.

"But he didn't care bout them boxes, cause
He was a-wearin seven coats all at the same time,
An he had on three-pairs o boots— but the worst thang was
He'd clean fergot his own name!"

"Pea-brained idjit!" Alice continued, as if she was the chorus.

"He'd answer to "Hey you!" or any loud shout,
Like "Danged Yankee!" or "Bee's Wax!"
Or "Moon over Bama!" or "Bad-to-the Bone!"
But specially to "Whatchamacallit!"

"But iffen you preferred a more forceful one,
He even had more names than them:
His drinkin buds callt him 'Sweet Tater Pie,'
And his enemies, 'Hominy Grits.'

"His body was puny—and his IQ was low—"
(So the Bellman would often complain)—
"But he was right brave, and after all, that's what matters
When you come face te face with a Snark."

"He'd joke with hyeenas, an stare right back at em
Whilst he was a-waggin his haid,
And once't he even held hands with a bear,
"Jest to keep its spirits up," he said."

"You cain't walk hand-in-hand with no bear," Alice interrupted.

"Why not?"

"They ain't got hands, Bubba. They's got paws."

"Same thang!"

"'Tain't!"

"Okay. Let's jest say that they walked hand-in-paw then. That suit you?"

Alice laughed and tickled him in the ribs again. "Yeah. That's better."

"You might want to write Mr Lewis Carroll and complain bout his poem," Bubba suggested.

"Won't do no good," Alice responded.

"Why not? He might listen."

"He's daid, Bubba. He ain't readin no letters anymore."

"Oh. When'd that happen?"

"Probly a hunnert years ago—at least."

"In that case, you're probly right. You want me to go on?"

Alice reached over and gave him a light peck on the cheek. "Yes, Bubba, dear. Please *do* go on."

Alice's sugar, the moon, and the jasmine were beginning to make Bubba's head swim, but he went on as best he could remember the poem:

"He come along as a Cook, but finally allowed as how—
And this like to drove the Bellman half-mad—
That he could only bake weddin cakes—and whut was bad was,
They hadn't brung even one uv the fixins."

"That must'a been a big disappointment fer that am-oh-russ bear," Alice interjected.

"Which bear?"

"The one what he was holdin paws with—the one he was sweet on."

"They was jest friens, Alice. He didn't want to git hitched with it! Good grief!"

Alice laughed. "You never know. Thar's some purty odd fellers out thar."

Bubba shook his head. "No guy's ever goin to marry no bear! No way! Anyway,

"The last o the crew needs some extry explainin
In spite o lookin like some kind o dummy;

He's jest got this one idee, see—but that one's "Snark",
So the Bellman hires him right on the spot."

"I ain't real sure which one of them is the stupidest," Alice observed; "him or that Bellranger."

Bubba ignored her and went on:

"He come as a Butcher; but he finely let on,
After they'd been sailin fer at least a week,
That he only killt beavers. Naturally, this skeered the Bellman..."

"To say nothin bout that poor beaver!" Alice observed, her eyes as wide as Moon Pies at this shocking news.

Bubba nodded, then added:

"He was most too skeered to even speak."

"Anybody best think twice't afore they go killin any o ma pets!" Alice allowed. "I'll be all over em like white on a golf ball. Blieve me, I'll whup the livin tar out of em!"

"I'll keep that in mind," Bubba said, grinning like a possum. "But the next time that dang cat o yours attacks ma ankles I jest might be tempted."

Alice punched him hard in the ribs with a surprisingly powerful left jab.

"Ow!" Bubba protested. "I was jest funnin! You probly broke one o ma ribs!"

"I doubt it!" Alice said. "A big ole ex-lineman like you? I doubt even a mule could do that with a swiff kick." She reached over and gently rubbed where she had punched him. "Thar, Honeybunch. That feel better?"

Bubba grinned from ear to ear. "Not yet. Keep on a-rubbin."

Alice punched him again.

Bubba yelped and then laughed loudly as he tried to kiss her, but she pushed him away. "I ain't kissin on some guy what's threatnin to kill ma cat! Git on with your dang poem an quit pawin at me!" She said all of this while smiling a most enticing smile that told Bubba that she really didn't mind.

Bubba continued:

"After a bit the Captain explained, in a trimblin tone,
"We only got the one beaver on board;
An that one's my own dear pet,
Whose death would be deeply deplored."

As it happened, the Beaver overheard this remark,
An its eyes welled up with tears,
Sayin that "Even the rupture o huntin a Snark,…"

"Rupture?" Alice asked. "Jest how heavy is one o them Snarks?"

Bubba thought for a moment. "Maybe the word was 'rapture'; not 'rupture'."

Alice laughed. "Big differnce, Bubba!"

He grinned. "Yeah. What a differnce a vowel makes!"

They both laughed hard.

"I reckon it's 'rapture'," Bubba said. "Lemme try that one agin:

Sayin that 'Even the rapture o huntin a Snark,
Cain't make up fer that dismal surprise!'

The Beaver tells the Captain that the Butcher should
Make the trip in his own ding-dang boat:
But the Captain says that this'd never fit
With the plans he'd made fer their trip.

Navigation's always been hellaciously hard
Even fer jest one ship an one bell,
An he wasn't about to try
To undertake it with two boats as well.

Now, no doubt the best thang this Beaver could do
Would be to git him a bullet-proof vest,
An the Cook tole the Beaver it should git
Him a life insurance policy as wall.

Still, ever after that miserable day
When the Butcher was somewhar close by,
The Beaver kept lookin t'other way,
An seemed uncomfortbly shy.

That's the end o the first fit."

"The end o the first what?" Alice asked.

"The first 'fit'. That's what the chapters're callt: 'fits'. The poem's a 'agony in eight fits'."

"What kind o fits?" Alice asked, still not understanding. "Bare knuckle fits or crazy fits?"

"Crazy fits, I'm a-thinkin."

"So thar's seven more o these fits te go?"

"Yep, but I don't recall all seven. You want te hear a few more verses?"

"Mebbe a few, I guess. Are there any excitin parts? Tell me one what's got somethin about a snark in it."

"Wall, let's see. Thar's somethin interestin in the second fit—about how to recognize a snark. You want to hear that?"

"Yeah, go ahead. That might be useful in case I was te see one waltzin down the middle o the street or somethin."

Bubba laughed. "Ther's not too likely; still, I reckon you never know. This here's the five unmistakable signs of gen-u-ine Snarks:

"Let's take em in order. The first un's its taste
Which is meager an hollow, but crisp..."

"Sounds like a tater chip te me!" Alice observed.

"Yeah, a bit," Bubba agreed.

"Like a coat what's a few sizes too small,
With a flavor of Will-o-the-Wisp."

"Now, I've tasted all sorts o tater chips—Bar-B-Q, Ranch Dressin, an even Vinegar an Dill Pickle—but I ain't never tried no Will-o-the-Wisp tater chips!"

"You like Doritos?" Bubba asked, getting off of the subject while thinking about snacks.

"I jest *love* Doritos! They's bodaciously good with a cold RC!"

"Shoot, Alice! You think everthin's good with a RC!"

"Most things are," agreed Alice. "Even you, Bubba!" She took a sip of her RC, then reached over and kissed him full on the mouth and let a little RC seep onto his tongue.

"Ummmm! That's real good!" Bubba declared. "More!" said Bubba, puckering up.

"Not now! I wanna hear bout them snarks."

Bubba frowned, but was encouraged about the possibility that there might be a little more sugar later, so he continued. "This is the second way:

"It's in the bad habit o gittin up late,
Which it carries quite a bit too far.
Sometimes it ets breakfast at suppertime,
An then supper the follerin day!"

"Why, that souns jest like you, Bubba!" exclaimed Alice, poking him the ribs again. "You a snark in disguise?"

"No, I ain't no snark! An here's how you kin tell that I ain't, cause I can take a joke:

"The third way is that it cain't take a joke.
Iffen you try to pull one over on it,
It'll sigh like a thang what's got all depressed:
An it simply cain't abide no puns.

"The fourth is its fondness fer bathin-machines,…"

"Fer what?" Alice demanded.

"Bathin-machines."

"What's that?"

"I'm not right sure. I guess snarks must like jacuzzis an hot tubs."

"If that makes you a snark then mebbe I'm part snark," Alice said. "That's one o ma dreams—havin a hot tub out on the back deck. That soun like fun to you, Bubba?"

"Yeah—iffen you're in it!"

Alice squeezed his bicep. "You git one, Bubba, an I'll come over an play in it with you."

"I might jest do that! Anyway, like I was a-sayin:

"The fourth is its fondness fer bathin-machines,
Which it likes to carry about,
Cause it believes that they add te the beauty o scenes—
But not evryone likely agrees.

"The fifth one's ambition—whatever that is.
Now to describe the two kinds that there are:
Thar's them what's got feathers, and bite,
And them what's got whiskers, and scratch."

"These common Snarks don't do any harm,…"

"Bitin an scratchin don't soun exactly harmless to me," Alice observed. "Unless it's from a puppy, I spose."

"You skeered yet?" Bubba asked.

"Harly! So far you ain't tole me bout nothin but a lil scratchin an bitin. Shoot, most folks do that while they're havin a cuddle. Tell me somethin bout them Boojum snarks—the ones what's supposed to be so all-farred dangerous."

"Okay. That's in the third fit, whar the Cook's a-makin a little speech, tellin his buds bout what his dear ole uncle once't tole him bout Snarks, jest afore he kicked the bucket. This here's what he sez:

"'Iffen yer Snark be a Snark, that's all right:..."

"Whatcha spose he meant by that?" Alice asked. "Iffen it's a Snark then o course it's a Snark! This guy's dumber'n a stump!"

"I know; I know," said Bubba. "Some o the poem's right silly. Jest let me finish the verse, will you?"

Alice apologized. "I'm, sorry, Bubba, I know it ain't your fault fer soundin so stupid-like. You go on ahead. Here—have nother sip o ma RC to whet your whistle."

Bubba took a sip. "Uummm! That's good. I sure wisht you hadn't et all the Moon Pies afore I got here."

"You know me! I cain't control maself when thar's Moon Pies around. When you git done with this here Snark poem you got to take me te git some o them pies. You hear?"

"I promise. Now, like I was a-sayin:

"'Iffen yer Snark be a Snark, that's all right:
Fetch it on home cause you can serve it with greens,
An it's right handy fer strikin a light."

"What kind o greens?" Alice wanted to know, always interested in recipes.

"The poem don't say. I spose any greens'd do fine: collard greens, poke greens, wild onions, ramps—"

"How bout kudzu?"

"I reckon kudzu'd do fine, too. You ever et any kudzu?"

"Why sure! Kudzu's good—iffen you fix it raight. Most folks don't even know it's good etin. But it is. Can I ast you one other thang, while I've got you all interrupted and everthin?"

"Sure. You kin ast me anythin, anytime."

"How you figger a Snark's good fer strikin a light?"

Bubba thought for a moment. "Wall, it might be like a dragon and have fire a-comin out o its mouth sometimes. Then agin, it might jest have real rough skin, sort o like sandpaper."

"Thank you, Bubba. I was jest a mite curious bout that."

"You're welcome. The next verse is a bit puzzlin, so don't ast me to explain it, cause I cain't. It tells you how te go bout huntin fer a Snark:

> *"You can look fer it with thimbles—and hunt it with care—"*

Alice burst out laughing. "Why you need a dang thimble? Yer Snark got a hole tore in it and need mendin?" She laughed some more, unable to control herself thinking about 250-pound, six-foot-three Bubba with a thimble on his finger, searching around in the brambles and vines for a snark with a hole in it.

Bubba laughed with her, enjoying her company. "I know! This part's real silly. Mebbe it's got a hole in its sock or somethin, I don't know."

This made Alice laugh all the harder, thinking about a big fire-breathing dragon stomping around the countryside in its stocking-feet with one of its big toes sticking out. It was a little while before they both quit laughing and Bubba could continue:

"You can hunt fer it with forks an hope…"

"Wall, that at least makes a mite more sense!" Alice allowed. "Least-wise you'd be ready to start ettin it once't you caught it!"

Bubba nodded.

"You can threaten to whomp its haid with a railroad tie,
An you can charm it with smiles an soap—"

"That sounds jest like Momma. She always tole me that the best way to charm somebody was to smile and wash-up real good, so's you smell sweet." She smiled and snuggled up against him. "You like how I smell, Sugar?"

Bubba buried his face in her hair and took a deep breath. "Uummmm! You smell good nuff to et," he said. "I'm charmed right out o ma britches!"

'Git back in them britches!"Alice demanded, and then took a few nibbles on his earlobe before asking, "What'd his uncle have te say bout huntin fer Boojums?"

"We're gittin te the skeery part now. This is what he says bout that:

"But look here, Boy, you best beware o the day,
Iffen yer Snark's a Boojum! Fer then
You're goin te softly an suddenly vanish,
An we ain't never goin te hear from you agin!"

"This here's what oppresses ma soul,
When I thinks bout ma Uncle's last words:
An my heart's like nothin more'n a big bowl
Full o jiggly, wiggly Jell-O!"

"What kinda Jell-O?" Alice immediately asked.

"He don't say. Could be any kind, I reckon."

"I'm partial to lime Jell-O, with crushed pineapple an cottage cheese in it. What's your favorite?"

"I like lime, too. And I'm right fond o cranberry, with lil bits o apple, an celry, and chopped nuts in it. You don't seem too skeered bout that Boojum makin you vanish an all."

"Naw! I ain't skeered—jest as long as it ain't got no chainsaw an it ain't wearin no hockey mask, o course!"

"Yer purty brave—fer a girl."

Alice punched him hard in the ribs again. "What you mean 'fer a gurl'?"

Bubba laughed. "You keep it up an I'm goin te have a bunch o big ole bruises. That lil fist o yours feels like gettin poked by the end o a two-by-four!"

"Awhhh! The big ole football player's sensitive!"

Bubba grinned. "How'd you like me te poke you in them skinny lil ribs o yours with ma fanger? See how you like it."

"You do an I'll pour this here RC all over your haid! We'll see how you like that!"

"Don't you go wastin no good RC, you hear now?"

"You're jest skeered you'll have te go warsh the sticky out o your precious burr-cut hair!" Alice acted like she was going to pour her pop on top of his head. He grabbed her arm and while he was holding it stole a quick kiss. Alice liked it, but poked him the ribs again anyway.

"You stop that and finish that poem!" she demanded, grinning all the time.

"Let's see. I'm wonderin what part to tell you next. You want to hear bout the Jubjub Bird? That's over in the fifth fit."

"Where'd the Jubjub Bird come from?" Alice asked. "You didn't mention him."

"The Jubjub Bird lives on the same island as Snarks. You wannah hear bout it or not?"

"Sure. Go ahead. It souns fascinatin." She rolled her eyes.

"As to tempermunt the Jubjub's a desprate bird,
Cause it lives in perpetual passion—"

Sortta like you, I reckon," Bubba interjected to make this observation.

"That's why you like me," Alice countered. "I'm all full o passion. Go on—admit it!"

"That's true nuff," Bubba admitted. "That an you like Moon Pies." He continued:

"Its taste in costumes is jest plain absurd—
It's ages ahead o the fashion."

"But it knows any frien that it's met once't afore:
An it won't even look at a Toy-oh-tah:
An at charity balls it stans at the door,
An collects all the money in a can.

"When you cooks one it's more better by far
Than chittlins, catfish, or shrimp:
Some folks think it's best kept in a jar,
But others put it straight in the freezer.

"You're spose'd te boil it with sawdust, an salt it with glue:..."

This caused Alice to break into hysterics, but Bubba ignored her and just kept on going:

"You steam it with grasshoppers and kudzu:
Whilst tryin yer dead-level best
To preserve its beautiful shape."

"I don't think thars much danger o Jubjub Birds ever takin the place o turkey at Thanksgivin!" Alice remarked. "I can hear it now: 'Whut's in this interestin stuffin, Honeybun?' 'Why that's boiled sawdust, Sugah! You want a second helpin?'"

This cracked Bubba up and the two of them laughed until their sides hurt.

"I tole you this poem's funny!" Bubba said, tears of laughter running down his cheeks.

"Yer right bout that! Say, I was jest wonderin bout somethin—what ever happent to that shy Beaver?"

"You're goin to find this hard to believe, but the Butcher and Beaver became close friends."

"No way!" Alice protested.

Bubba shrugged. "Go figger. Still, it's true. Here's what it says in the poem:

"Sech friens, as the Beaver and Butcher became,
Have seldom, if ever, been known;
In winter or summer, it's all jest the same—
You always finds em together.

"An iffen once't in awhile they git into a spat—this sometimes
Happens between even the closest of friens—
The horrible shriek o the Jubjub comes to thar minds,
An cements their frienship ferever!"

"That's real sweet!" Alice observed. "I was kinda worried bout that lil beaver. How bout that horrible Boojum? Them boys ever run into one o those?"

"As a matter o fact they do. That's in the last agonizin fit. That's number eight. It goes somethin like this:

They shuddered te think that they might lose the chase,
An the Beaver, real excited an all,
Went a-boundin along on the tip o its tail,
Fer the daylite was a-fadin right fast.

"Listen! I can hear Whatchamacallit a-shoutin!" the Bellman said,
"He's shoutin his fool haid near clean off!
An he's wavin his hans, and a-waggin his haid;
He's found him a Snark, that's fer sure!"

They looked in delight, while the Butcher exclaimed,
"He's always been a real Good Ole Boy!"
They watched him—their Cook—their hero an all—
Along the top o a neighborin ridge.

Standin tall and composed, fer one moment o time,
But in the next, that wild figger they saw
(As if stung by a bee) plunge into the sea,
While they waited and listened in awe.

"It's a Snark!" was the words that first hit their ears,
Which seemed most too good te be true,
Then follered a torrent o laughter an cheers:
Then the omnous words "It's a Boo—"

Then, NOTHIN. Some boys fancied they heared in the air

A most wearisome sigh
That sounded like "—jum!" but the others thought
It was only the breeze that blew by.

They hunted till dark was upon em, but they didn't
Find even a button or a feather
By which they could tell whar the Cook had been
standin
When the Cook had met with the Snark.

In the midst o the word he'd been tryin te say,
In the midst o his laughter an glee,
He'd softly an suddenly vanished away—
Fer the Snark was a Boojum, you see."

Bubba paused.

"That it?" Alice asked.

"Yep. The End!"

"You're right, Bubba," Alice allowed. "The endin's right skeery."

Bubba grinned. "I warn't you! But it's funny, too."

"You know what would'a made it skeerier?" Alice asked.

"What's that?"

"Iffen the Boojum would'a jumped out from behind a big rock a-holdin a chainsaw that's a-buzzin!"

Afterword

Now, before you get on my case about making fun of the South, I need to tell you about several of my great-grandfathers. One of them, on my father's side, owned a farm in Texas. During the Civil War he joined Wall's Legion to fight for the Confederacy, and was at the fall of Vicksburg, Mississippi. According to my father, who wrote a short history of his direct family line, this particular great-grandfather was wounded three times, and almost starved to death, subsisting on mules and rats during the siege. I have a daguerreotype of him in his Civil War uniform, holding his rifle, which was almost as tall as he was. If you look close you can see that he's holding his pants up with a belt fastened with a Union buckle. Another great-grandfather, this one on my mother's side, also lived in Texas at the time, out in the western frontier near San Angelo. He was in the Texas Cavalry, posted at Fort Concho, along with his older brother. They were participants in a tragic battle with Indians they mistook for Kiowas, called The Battle of Dove Creek, where he was wounded in the face and his brother was killed. He almost died when they got lost in a three-day blizzard trying to make their way back to the fort with the wounded. All in all, it's a small wonder that I even exist. I only tell you these things so that you know I have some Southern roots. Of lesser import is the fact that I have drunk my fair share of Royal Crown Cola, eaten a few Moon Pies, and consumed at least my weight in Milky Way Bars, though I must admit that I prefer Snickers.

Byron W. Sewell
June 2014

In the Boojum Forest

In the Boojum Forest

The first hint I had of the possible existence of a dwarf variety of the famous Boojum tree was when I spotted a packet of six seeds offered on eBay with a "Buy It Now" price of $30. I sent an e-mail message to the seller, who went by the name of SonoraPete42, and asked him if he could provide details about where the seeds had come from and why he believed them to be a legitimate dwarf variety and not just from a stunted or diseased specimen.

He responded:

> I purchased these six seeds in Sonoyta, Sonora from Miguel Martínez, who owns and operates a medicinal herb shop on the main plaza. I have dealt with him for many years and I trust him. He told me that he had obtained the seeds from a Yaqui *brujo* (or shaman) named Woi Taka Woi, who collects psychotropic plants in the Sonora Desert in Mexico. This *brujo* is said to have traveled widely in Northern Mexico and Baja California, and to be well acquainted with ordinary Boojum trees. Woi told Martínez that he came across a number of mature and healthy dwarf specimens on top of a mesa, none of which were taller than eight feet, and that he collected these seeds from those plants. I believe them to be quite rare. Martínez also made a point that he could not guarantee that they would germinate, so we are unable to do so either. We have a strict "no refund" policy. If you decide

to purchase them you will be buying them "dead or alive". Thank you for checking out our site. Peder Wagner.

I was intrigued enough by what appeared to be the seeds from some floral outlaws with a price on their heads to buy them. After all, one doesn't often have the opportunity to discover a new desert plant variety in his lifetime. I figured the seeds were worth the $30 asking price if even one of them germinated, since I could easily sell it for $500 to any number of people I knew in Tucson and Phoenix who collected rare desert plants.

I was quite familiar with the ordinary Boojum tree, though "ordinary" was probably something of a misnomer, since each plant was likely as unique and recognizable as the unique patterns on the flukes of sperm whales. Many mature specimens had such bizarre shapes that it was even sometimes difficult to believe that they were members of the same species. A few extraordinary specimens had even been given names and were well-known by people who loved the desert and were intimately familiar with it. I had seen hundreds of these crazy trees when I had taken an extended trip to Baja several years ago to study its unique flora, a trip that had involved a very close call with a rattlesnake that I had almost stepped on. One thing that I learned from that expedition was to wear snake-proof boots when searching for Boojums.

It is quite common for a mature Boojum to reach a height of 20 to 30 feet, and there is even a reported specimen in an isolated and protected area in Mexico that is said to tower to 80 feet. That height seems unlikely, but that is the claim. Estimates of the age of such a giant are in the 700- to 800-year range. Obviously, they grow very slowly, probably no more than an inch or two a year, depending upon the amount of moisture in the monsoons and coastal fogs. I have a nice specimen growing in my backyard here in Tucson that is about six feet tall and probably 50 years old. I doubt that I will live long enough to see it achieve 10 feet.

When the seeds arrived they looked badly desiccated and I was skeptical that any of them would germinate, but knowing that desert seeds can lie dormant for years awaiting moisture, I planted them in little pots and watered them every month. After waiting for six months without the appearance of a single sprout it was pretty obvious that I had paid $30 for a packet of dead seeds. I exhumed them and saved them anyway. Who knows? Perhaps in the future they can be cloned from their DNA.

Unwilling to just let my dreams of Dwarf Boojums simply wither away, I resolved to undertake an expedition to locate the Yaqui *brujo* and see if I could hire him to take me into the desert to see them in the wild for myself. I realized that such an endeavor would be expensive and probably dangerous. There would be the normal and expected hazards of the hostile environment, where almost everything could either sting, bite or pierce: cacti, wasps, spiders, poisonous snakes, and even poisonous lizards. There were also the even more hazardous dangers of lunatic Mexican drivers, corrupt local police (to say nothing of the reputed horrors of Mexican jails), and drug smugglers and growers. I could think of dozens of ways to end up dead (or worse) in the Sonora, and if this happened to me in some isolated spot out in the desert then it was pretty unlikely that anyone would come looking for me, much less ever find my sun-bleached remains.

I waited until early March, when the weather had moderated, to travel to Sonoyta, heading west from Tucson towards Why (which in retrospect seemed like a legitimate question), and then turned south across the Organ Pipe National Monument to the Port of Entry at Lukeville on the monument's southern boundary. The town of Sonoyta itself

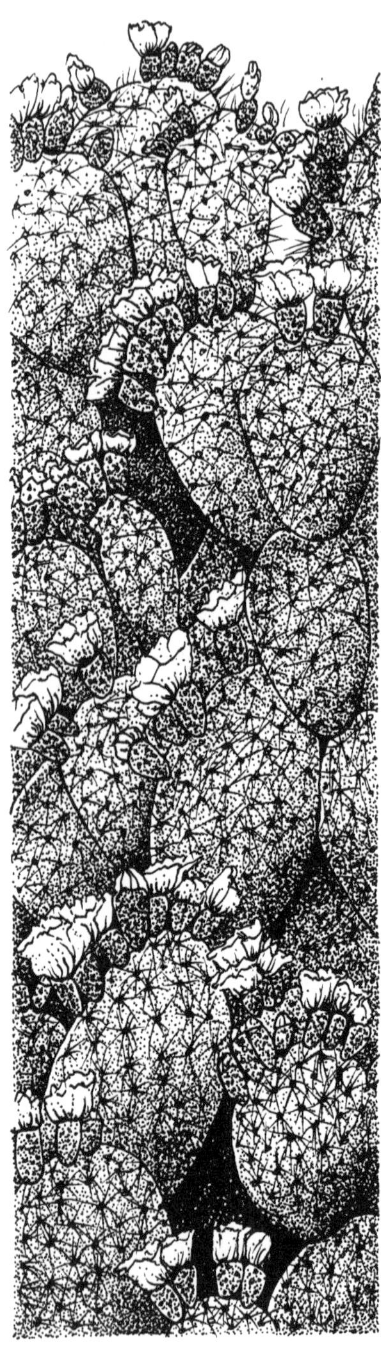

was a few miles further south across the border. Locating Martínez's shop on the main plaza was no problem, since he had done business there for decades and was well known. The first local resident I asked for directions turned out to be one of his cousins, who took me to his shop.

Martínez's shop had a small frontage on the plaza and went back for at least thirty feet. The complex, bitter and pungent odor of a mixture of many different dried desert plants almost knocked me over when I stepped inside. This was certainly not somewhere that a person with allergies should venture. After taking just a few breaths I felt lightheaded, with the same buzz than one might expect from a deep toke on a marijuana cigarette. Bundles of dried plants were everywhere. Innumerable stacks of plants were piled on wooden shelves almost to the ten-foot ceiling. Shredded plants in little polyethylene bags filled dozens of baskets. Hundreds of upside-down bundles of plants were festooned from the rafters. It was dark inside compared to the blinding sunlight out in the plaza and it took a few moments for my eyes to adjust to the gloom. I finally spotted someone at the back of the shop working under the light streaming in from a small, high window and I made my way to where he was working behind an old display counter, sorting and wrapping plants. I spoke Spanish well enough that I didn't require a translator. "Good day, señor," I said. "My name is Rex Tannenholtz. I'm looking for Miguel Martínez."

"I am Miguel. What can I do for you?"

"I was wondering if you might know how to contact the *brujo* Woi Taka Woi?"

"Perhaps," he said, his voice suddenly laced with suspicion. "Why do you wish to speak to him?"

"I would like to offer him a job."

"He doesn't work. He is a religious man, who spends his time alone in the desert. He would not be interested."

"I think that he might. Some months ago I purchased a packet of seeds on eBay for what was reputed to be a dwarf variety of the Boojum tree. I planted them, but they did not germinate. The seller told me that he had obtained these seeds from you."

Miguel was immediately on the defensive. "I do not offer a warranty for desert seeds, señor. I cannot guarantee that they will germinate. I am not God."

"I did not expect that you would do that, and I'm not here to make any claim on you. I bought the seeds at my own risk, and I am not saying that you did anything wrong or that you owe me anything." His expression noticeably relaxed. "The man who sold me the seeds told me that you had obtained them from the *brujo* Woi, who had collected them in Mexico, somewhere out in the Sonora Desert. I was hoping that you could put me into contact with him or tell me where I might find him. I would like to ask him to guide me to the plants that the seeds came from—I would pay him, of course."

"Woi is impossible to contact. As I said, he spends most of his time wandering through the desert. There are no phones or post offices where he goes, and very few humans either, for that matter. Most people could not survive out there for even a day. He has never told me the name of his village. I simply see him when he walks through the shop door to offer me something for sale."

"How often is that?"

"A few times a year. I am never sure when it will be, though he usually comes through Sonoyta around Lent or Easter. I think that he takes plants to the Pascua Yaqui who have a small reservation north of Tempe, for use in the *maso bwikam*, the 'Deer Dance', for which they are deservedly famous."

"I am familiar with these people. Most members of the American tribe now live in Guadalupe." I reached into my shirt pocket and took out a postcard that I had brought. I handed it to him. "Perhaps I could leave you this postcard. It is addressed to me and ready to mail. You can see that I have put a Mexican stamp on it. If you would simply write a date on it to let me know when he might be in Sonoyta I would be very grateful. I would come back and spend a few days and see if I might be able to meet him. I feel sure that I can make it worth his while to guide me to the dwarf Boojum trees."

Miguel didn't look too excited about doing this, so I took out a ten dollar bill and placed it on the countertop. "This should compensate you for the trouble of taking this very heavy postcard all the way across the big plaza to the post office."

He took the bill. "All right. I will see if I can help you, but I cannot promise anything. Like I told you, Woi only comes into my shop on rare occasions. It might even be a year or more until the next time I see him. What's more, he is old and could even be dead."

"How old?"

"I don't know. I doubt if he even knows himself. I would guess maybe 60 or 70. But he spends his life out-of-doors and the weather and sun are hard on a person's skin. He could be much younger; only God knows."

I nodded. "I understand. When—and if—you see him next time please tell him that I will pay him five hundred American dollars in cash to guide me to the trees."

Miguel's eyebrows shot up and he looked at me as if he thought I had been smoking jimson weed. "That is a great deal of money, señor Rex!"

I nodded.

He turned the postcard over to look at the picture. "What is this drawing?"

"It is from an old English book of poetry, entitled *The Hunting of the Snark*. It's by an illustrator named Henry Holiday. What you see is a character named The Bellman, who is the captain of the ship that you can see in the distance. He is leading an expedition to search for snarks."

"Is he about to scalp the little man?"

"No, he is holding him up so that his feet will not get wet in the surf. He is ringing a bell, not wielding a club."

"It looks very painful to avoid getting his feet wet. What are snarks?"

"They are mythical creatures, said to be very delicious. However, one variety of snark is very dangerous. If you encounter it you vanish without a trace."

"Which kind might that be?"

"It's called a Boojum. That is what the Boojum tree was named after."

"Really?"

I nodded.

"That's very interesting. I would like to read this poem. Is it available in Spanish?"

"Yes, but it is hard to find copies. If you are able to contact Woi for me I will find a copy and send it to you. This will take some time, however, since I will have to order it from Spain."

He smiled. "I will find Woi for you. I would like to read this book. It sounds very funny."

"Yes; many people find it to be amusing."

On the way back to Tucson I spent the afternoon visiting Organ Pipe Monument, enjoying the cacti—until I was stung on the back of my neck. I hate desert wasps!

Three weeks later the postcard arrived in my mailbox. Inscribed on it was simply: "*Marzo* 27–31". That was only two days away, so I quickly packed a suitcase and returned to Sonoyta the next day. I went directly to Miguel's shop.

"I received the postcard," I told him. "Thank you."

"You are welcome."

"When did you see Woi?"

"A week ago. He was on his way through the wire to Guadalupe with a bag of peyote buttons. He told me that he planned to come back through Sonoyta sometime between March 27 and 31. However, I cannot promise that he will show up during those dates. He has a different concept of time that normal people do. Sometimes it seems to stop for him. It could easily be a few weeks later. If he goes into a trance then he can be in such a state for days at a time."

"I understand. Did you explain to him why I wanted to see him?"

"Yes. He seemed interested after I told him that you would be willing to pay him $500. That is more money than he makes in an entire year—even selling peyote to the Navajo and Cheyenne—which brings a good price on the reservations."

I nodded. "Thank you for your help. I will be staying at the Hotel Coronado across the plaza. If he shows up would you please come and find me?" I placed a $20 bill on the counter.

He picked it up. "Of course. It will be my pleasure."

I sat around the hotel drinking Coronas and margaritas, eating simple but excellent Mexican cuisine, and reading several paperback novels that I had brought with me. The end of March finally arrived, but Woi never showed. I left Miguel another postcard and a ten-dollar bill, and returned to Tucson that evening, a bit disappointed, but not surprised.

I walked into my house a little after 10:00 p.m. and turned off the alarm system. When I flicked on a light in the living room I was startled to find a small, wiry man with a classic Indian face standing in front of the coffee table. He wore a white cotton shirt and pants, and simple sandals.

My first reaction was that I had come in on a burglar. "What are you doing in my house?" I demanded in Spanish.

"My name is Woi Taka Woi," he said in very calm Spanish. "I understand that you wish to see the little Boojums."

"Oh!" I said. "I'm sorry. You startled me. I thought you might be a burglar! How did you get in here without setting off the alarm?" It was a sophisticated alarm system, but it obviously wasn't sophisticated enough.

"I came down the chimney. It has no alarm."

I laughed. I couldn't help it. A strange image of him dressed up like Santa Claus with a bag full of peyote slung over his shoulder flashed through my mind. "Down the chimney?"

"Yes."

This was crazy. The flue was quite small. "There's no soot on your clothing," I observed as if that were proof he had done no such thing.

"I took the form of a bat," he said calmly. "A bat can easily come down your chimney without getting covered in soot."

"A bat?" I said, not comprehending what he was saying. I laughed again; I couldn't help it. This guy was very funny.

"Yes," he said with a straight face. "Brown Bat is one of my totem animals."

It suddenly dawned on me what he was telling me. He was claiming that he had shape-shifted into a bat in order to come down my chimney. I decided to play along, even though I didn't believe a word of what he was saying and suspected that he had actually found an unlocked window. "How did you know where I live?"

"Miguel told me. He had it written down on a postcard with a picture of a very ugly man who is about to scalp a little man."

"When did you see Miguel?"

"About two hours after you left Sonoyta. He told me that I had just missed you."

"But you beat me here! How is that possible?"

"I flew."

There was limited and very irregular private air service between Sonoyta and Tucson, but I found it hard to believe that he would have been able to take advantage of it. A ticket might well cost him more than his annual income. "By plane?" I asked.

He smiled, revealing perfect teeth. "No, señor. I could never afford such a thing. I am a poor man. And it would have been a waste of precious money, even if I had the price of the ticket, which I certainly do not."

"What do you mean then?"

"A bat is not delayed in crossing the border at Lukeville. A Bat can fly overhead and watch a person get stung on the neck by a wasp. A bat can fly the most direct route across the desert."

I stared at him, dumbfounded. He was obviously quite serious. How could he have known that I had been stung? And besides, I could think of no other possible explanation.

"Would you like a beer?" I asked trying to act nonchalant about such a fantastic claim. "You must be very tired after such a long flight."

"Yes, my arms are very tired. I would like a glass of water," he said. "Thank you."

"Of course." I went into the kitchen and returned with the water. "Are you hungry? I could fix you something. Perhaps some tortillas and beans? An apple?"

"No, thank you. That is very kind of you." He drank the water and handed the glass back to me.

"Please, sit down," I said, gesturing to the sofa and sitting the empty glass on top of the coffee table. He sat down and I sat down opposite him in a chair.

"What are your other totem animals?" I asked, very curious about this shaman.

"The Ant, the Javelina, and the Road Runner."

This didn't strike me as being a particularly powerful array of spirit animals. "Not a bear or a wolf? Or a mountain lion?"

"Size and strength can be deceiving," he said. "Such an animal as one of those is not always the one who can provide the kind of help that is needed most. If you are locked in a room, an ant can crawl under the door and bring help. Even a large bear might not be able to tear down the door if it is well made." He abruptly changed the subject. "When did you wish to search for the little Boojums?"

"As soon as possible. Before the desert gets too hot."

"Can you come to Bácum in four days' time?"

"Yes. I think so. I will need to rent an SUV and get enough supplies. How long will we be in the desert? I need to know how much to bring."

"Perhaps a week. I do not recall exactly where I found the Boojums, though I know approximately where they live. It is a very remote place and there are no roads through that part of the desert; only animal trails. We must walk. It will be dangerous. You must protect yourself from the cacti and animals that may wish to harm you. Wear chaps and thick boots. I would suggest that you bring a rifle or a pistol."

I nodded. "I am very familiar with the Sonora. I will come prepared. However, I don't think it is practical to carry enough water for the two us to last for a week. We would need a burro. Can you arrange to have one?"

"Just bring three canteens. I will find water."

"Are you absolutely certain? If you fail we might die."

"I am certain."

"How will I find you in Bácum?"

"You will see Raven sitting on the low wall surrounding the church on the main plaza. Follow Raven."

"Follow a raven?'

"Yes; he will bring you to me; out in the desert. He will know where I am."

"What if the raven flies ahead and I lose sight of him?"

"He will not leave you. Just follow."

I obviously had a doubtful expression.

"I would like to have the apple now," he said.

I stood up. "Of course; just a moment." I went back into the kitchen to get it. When I returned I saw a small brown bat circling the room at a very fast speed. With a sudden dive it flew into the fireplace and disappeared up the chimney. I couldn't help thinking of him as "Father Woi, the Christmas Bat."

Four days later I arrived in Bácum. I had come prepared with everything Woi had suggested, but also with a compass, a handheld GPS location device, and a cell phone. I parked the SUV on the edge of the plaza and found a policeman, whom I bribed to watch the vehicle while I was gone for $50. I collected my backpack and rifle, strapped on my chaps and walked over towards the church to look for a raven. I was not at all confident that I would find one, since ravens were not common in this part of Mexico, but to my pleasant surprise he was there, just as Woi had said that he would be. I walked up to the bird, standing no more than six feet away. It peered intently at me, as if trying to decide whether I was the right person or an imposter, and then lifted off, flying to a large cottonwood about a block down from the plaza on a dirt road that looked as if it led into the desert. I set off at a steady pace, and as soon as I was about twenty feet away the raven took wing again and flew another hundred feet and perched on a fence post, waiting for me to catch up. We traveled in this way, with the bird flying to another place to alight and me catching up. We hadn't traveled very far when I noticed that we were being shadowed by a lone coyote, which I found odd, since all

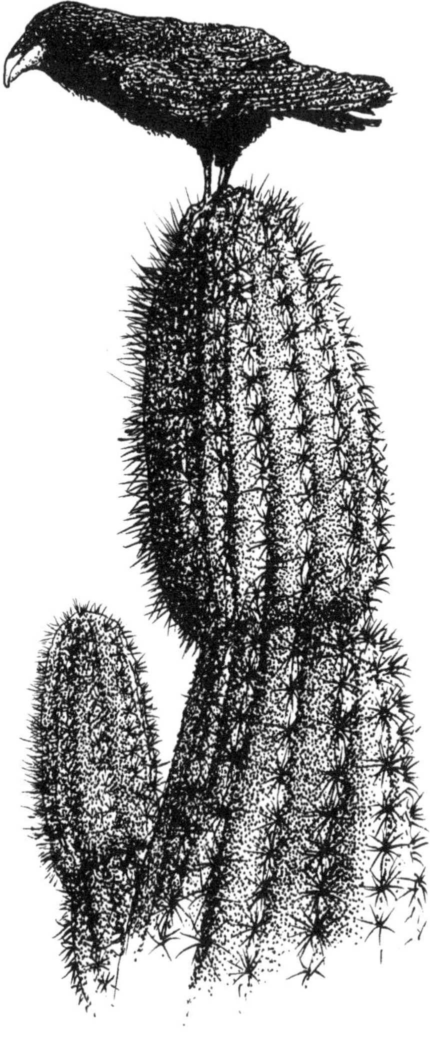

coyotes I have ever encountered are understandably wary of humans and run away when they spot one. We traveled this way for three hours and I finally sat down in the shade of an Ironwood tree in a dry wash to take a break. The raven flew back to where I was seated and perched on a high limb in the tree to wait for me.

I rested for ten minutes and then got back up, at which time the raven took wing again. We continued to travel this way for several more hours, the raven flying ahead and the coyote shadowing our trail. Then, to my dismay, the raven took wing and flew off, leaving me alone in the desert. I retrieved my GPS and checked to see where I was. We had traveled about ten miles. I had no idea what to do next, so I simply sat down on a rock in the shade of two ancient Saguaros, with their arms up as if being arrested by the Cactus Police, and waited. Ten minutes later Woi emerged from the chaparral and came over to where I was seated. He was dressed in the same clothes that I had seen him wearing when I found him in my living room, though this time he also had a serape over one shoulder and was carrying a machete. I had to admit that I was relieved to see him, even though I was confident that I could have made my way back to Bácum with the help of my compass and GPS.

"I see that you were able to follow Raven," he said.

"Yes, he was easy to follow. He even waited for me when I became tired and needed a short rest."

"Yes, I saw you as you rested under the ancient Ironwood tree."

This caught me by surprise. "How did you see me?"

"When I am in the Otherworld I can see through Raven's eyes—though the image is not as clear as my own vision. It is as if I were looking through water with sunshine streaming through it—as one might see the world if one is a fish."

I didn't know whether to believe him or not, but he seemed to know where I had sat down to rest. I had only seen the one Ironwood tree. I considered that this might have just been a good guess, since shade was hard to find in the desert; still it was unnerving to think that someone might be watching me through the eyes of a desert creature. Frankly, it made me a bit paranoid.

"Where did the raven go?" I asked.

"His task was done, and he was probably hungry."

"Where will we spend the night?" I asked. I wasn't at all excited about sleeping out in the open on the desert floor. Creepy things came out at twilight—tarantulas, snakes, and scorpions.

"There is a spring about two miles in that direction," he said, pointing to the north. "We will spend the night there. We should go while there is still good light."

"Lead the way," I said. "I will be right behind you."

I was surprised that Woi was wearing neither boots nor chaps. Had I tried to walk through the chaparral as he was dressed my legs would have been quickly and painfully covered in cactus needles. Somehow he managed to stay just out of reach of the Jumping Chollas that littered the ground around the large Cholla stands that were abundant here.

As we were walking I once again caught a glimpse of the coyote trailing us, this time only about 30 yards back. I remarked to Woi, "A coyote has been following me ever since I left Bácum."

Woi stopped and turned to look back to where we had come from. I thought I detected a flash of concern pass across his stoic face. "The Trickster," he said. "We will have to be careful with him around." He turned and went ahead. I looked back again, but I couldn't catch sight of the coyote again.

It took us nearly two hours to make our way over the rough terrain to the location of the spring, whose exact location Woi identified by a relatively large palo verde that grew beside it. As we approached, a dozen white-wing doves flew out of the tree, the rush of air through their beating wings making a familiar whistling sound. The spring itself was almost unnoticeable. A trickle of water seeped out of a crevice in a rock wall that overhung and sheltered a small clearing, the water dripping into a small dammed-up area that created a very shallow pool. It contained at most a few gallons of water. I imagined that the flow was no more than a quart in an hour.

The pool looked manmade. "Did you position these rocks?" I asked, pointing to the circular array of small stones.

"No. My great-grandfather did; many, many years ago. It prevents the water from simply flowing down into the hot sand below where it would quickly disappear. Many times I have used this place. It has saved my life on more than one occasion, when no other water could be found."

I sat a canteen beneath the steady drip to let it slowly fill.

"How far will we need to walk tomorrow?" I asked.

"About ten miles, to where there is another spring. We will rest there tomorrow night."

"What if that spring has dried up?"

"It hasn't," he said calmly, as if he had just recently confirmed this.

"How far from there are the Boojums?"

He shrugged. "Perhaps another day's walk."

"Does anyone live out here in the desert?" I asked, gesturing with a swing of my arm.

"No, not in the sense you mean. There are a few *brujos* that pass through here at times, and some Yaqui who hunt for food or search for peyote. There are deer and rabbit in the desert. But no one can stay here for long periods of time or make a living. It isn't possible. Even cattle cannot survive here unless a well is dug for water for them to drink, and there is no well in this place. The water is too deep. There are only wild animals here." He paused. "They will not be too happy with us tonight."

"Why?"

"We are here by the water. They are too shy to come in to drink as long as *you* are here."

I fully understood that I was the problem and that they would not be inhibited from doing so if Woi was alone. "I wouldn't hurt them."

"I believe you, but the animals do not know you."

"Perhaps we could move away from the spring to sleep," I suggested. "Is there someplace we can go where we would be safe? I really don't want to sleep on the bare ground."

He looked up the hillside. "There is a rock ledge up there, about fifty feet above us. We could sleep up there. But we should check while there is still light—to be sure that there are no snakes there."

This seemed like a good plan; I've never been too fond of sleeping with snakes. I filled the other canteens from the pool, and then Woi led the way up the hillside. It was a hard climb and the ledge was almost inaccessible. Thankfully, it didn't harbor any snakes on this particular evening and we soon made ourselves comfortable—if you can call sitting on a rock as qualifying as comfort.

"You seemed worried about the coyote," I remarked.

"It is never a good sign that the Trickster is following you. He is no doubt up to no good. We must be wary."

"What could a coyote possibly do to harm us?" I patted my rifle. "I could simply shoot him if you think that he is dangerous to us. You could certainly kill him with your machete. The two of us might even be able to kill him with our bare hands. He is not a large coyote; just a skinny one. He looks hungry."

Woi smiled at me the way an adult might smile at an ignorant child who has said something foolish. I decided that there was no point in arguing the matter. I knew that my large-bore rifle could drop a bull moose in its tracks and I was a good shot, even at a running target. "What could the Trickster possibly be up to?" I asked. "We wish it no harm."

"That may be, but that does not mean than he means us no harm in return—or that someone is not using him to bring us harm."

"Who would want to do that?" I found the idea of someone controlling a coyote far-fetched at best. "Who would even know that we are out here in the desert?"

"I am not the only *brujo* who travels the desert. I have made enemies of some. There is especially one *bruja;* an old woman who hates me. Any of them would certainly bring me harm if given the opportunity and if I am not vigilant. It is dangerous in the Otherworld, where everyone strives for power. It is fortunate that you saw the Trickster. I have now been warned."

"I don't see how a lone, mangy coyote can harm us here on this high ledge. He could not possibly attack us here. A coyote is a bad climber."

"He has powers that you do not understand. We must be cautious tonight."

I decided that I was hardly in a position to argue animist theology with a shaman and so I let the subject drop. I produced two high-energy bars from my backpack and gave one to Woi for his evening meal. He ate it slowly, savoring the chocolate in the mix. Within minutes of finishing it he was asleep. I, on the other hand, was awake for the next three hours, listening to the night sounds, wondering which creatures were visiting the pool and what the mysterious coyote might be up to. About 10:00 an almost-full moon rose, lighting the chaparral in a faint pearly light. It was behind us on the opposite side of the rocky hill, so I couldn't see the familiar snark-in-the-moon—the winged Boojum sneaking up behind the hapless Baker. I was glad for the light. I hated staring into pitch darkness, trying to see what was making every little chirp, squeak or scratch.

I was brought out of a deep sleep by the sudden, loud "clang!" of a machete striking stone. I sat up too quickly and bumped my head on the overhang. I hadn't even realized that I had dozed off. "What!" I said.

"The Trickster," Woi replied as he reached down and picked up a now-headless rattler by the tail. He held it out over the edge of the ledge so I could see it against the indigo sky. It was easily six feet long and as thick as my forearm.

"Yikes!" I said. "That's no coyote!"

"No. Not now."

"Why did you call it the Trickster?"

"It shape-shifted," he said. "When you saw him he was Coyote. To come up here to the ledge he became Rattlesnake. As you observed, Coyote is a poor climber."

"Are you telling me that the coyote and this snake were one and the same animal?" I have a very open mind, but this struck me as being so far-fetched as to be unbelievable.

"I hope so, because then Coyote is dead as well. In any event, Rattlesnake was sent to kill me—or perhaps, even kill us both."

"Why would someone want to kill me?"

"I don't know. Perhaps it has something to do with the little Boojum trees."

"How did you know that the snake had come up onto the ledge? When I saw you last you were sound asleep."

"The Ants warned me; they are my protectors."

"How did they warn you?"

"The normal way; they bit me."

"They bit you? Didn't that hurt?"

"Of course, but their bites were nothing compared to what the lethal bite of this snake would have felt like." He let the headless snake drop into the brush beneath the ledge and then flicked the dismembered head off of the ledge with the tip of his machete. "The ants will feast on him tonight."

"You're saying that you believe that the ants intentionally bit you to wake you? That they saw the snake coming and they bit you to warn you?"

"Yes, that is what happened. The ants are my protectors. In this instance they were more powerful than that Rattlesnake. One might not naturally think that was so."

"But the ants could have simply been foraging at night. Just because you got bitten doesn't mean that they intentionally warned you of an approaching snake."

"I am alive. You are alive. The snake is dead. And they no longer bite me." He held up his arm so that I could see it clearly in the moonlight. It was almost black; covered in a swarm of ants.

"Are they biting you now?"

"No. Now there is no need. I am awake. Rattlesnake is dead."

It was hard to argue with. I checked my watch. It was 4:00 a.m.

We descended from the ledge at sunrise, back down to the pool to top off the canteens. Woi walked a little ways away from the pool and stopped to study something in the soft sand. I finished filling the canteens and went over to see what he was studying.

I wasn't happy with what I saw: a large, obviously reptilian footprint. I hadn't brought along a tape measure, but it was easily 12 inches in length and fearsomely clawed. If it was a lizard then it was a very large lizard. As far as I was aware there were no Komodo dragons in the Sonora.

"What is it?" I asked.

Woi was still studying it carefully. He stood up. "I don't know," he said. "It looks somewhat like Lizard or Gila Monster's foot in shape, but I have never seen one large enough to leave such a print."

Nor had I. In fact I had never even seen a normal-sized Gila monster. They were endangered and few were still alive. "Are we in danger?" I asked, feeling very apprehensive about the possibility of such a large lizard somewhere in the nearby chaparral.

"I don't know," he admitted. "I will consult the Otherworld to find out. For now, we go," he said and abruptly headed northeast through the brush in a very purposeful direction. I followed, trying to keep up with him. He was walking at a very fast pace, as if anxious to get as far away from the footprint as he could, the sooner the better.

An hour later we were walking up the wide riverbed of a dry wash, its undercut banks lined with stands of creosote and palo verde. Above the trees on the hillside were enormous clusters of Organ Pipe cactus and Joshua trees. As we turned a bend in the wash Woi suddenly stopped and put out his arm to indicate that I should stop. I looked up the riverbed and saw a cluster of five or six turkey vultures feeding on the dark carcass of some large animal, perhaps a cow, I thought.

"What is it?" I asked, speaking in a low voice that was nonetheless loud enough to spook the vultures that suddenly noticed us and took wing, loudly flapping their wings as they struggled to gain altitude, their bodies obviously heavy from gorging on whatever it was that they had been feeding on.

"I don't know. Something dead. We should not stay here. Whatever killed it may still be near."

I took the rifle off of my shoulder and put a shell in the chamber. "I'll take a quick look," I said and went forward. Woi stayed where he was, obviously reluctant to approach the carcass.

I could see that it was obviously a cow once I got close enough to see it better. The sand around the hapless beast was dark with absorbed blood. There was little meat left; mostly just skin and bone. What was disturbing was that there were dozens of footprints of the same lizard-like animal that we had seen earlier back at the spring. I stood up, scanning the chaparral and the trees lining the wash, my rifle at the ready in case something came charging out at one of us. I signaled for Woi to come over, pointing at the ground. He came, but you could tell that it was only reluctantly. I pointed at the prints.

He nodded. "Lizard," he said.

"No, not lizard," I replied. "There are no lizards large enough to make these tracks. This is something else; something much, much worse."

"Lizard," he repeated. "We go now. This way." He pointed with an outstretched arm and set out at a quick pace in that direction. I fell in behind, my rifle at the ready.

"Where are we headed?" I asked.

"Shelter," was all that he said.

He was walking fast and I had a difficult time keeping up. It was hard to believe that a man who was obviously in his 60s or 70s could walk so fast and not tire.

Four hours later we reached a mesa, whose steep sides formed a series of arroyos on whose slopes were a virtual forest of Saguaros and Boojum trees. Woi headed up the slope of one arroyo whose sides were strewn with large boulders from an enormous rockslide that had probably happened centuries ago. About two-thirds the way up to the summit he slipped behind a particularly large slab of rock signaling that I should follow. He got down on his stomach and wriggled through a low gap. “Give me your rifle and backpack,” he said. I slipped them through to him and then wriggled through after them. The slab, at least six feet thick and as large as a one-car garage, was propped up against other huge chunks of rock, forming a space with a roughly triangular cross-section, which was just large enough to accommodate two people. There was enough room to sit but not nearly large enough room to stand up. Narrow gaps at the perimeter allowed enough light to enter to see easily once my eyes had adjusted to the darkness.

“We are safe here,” he said, “unless Lizard is small enough to crawl through the opening. But I think he is not. It would take a big lizard to kill an animal as big as a cow.”

“If it sticks its head through the opening then I will blow it off,” I said, patting my rifle. I handed him a canteen and got an energy bar for each of us out of my backpack. “What shall we do now?” I asked.

“We wait to see if Lizard is stalking us. I expect that he is.”

“It’s not a lizard,” I insisted. “There are no big lizards roaming the chaparral; there are no surviving dinosaurs.”

“It is obvious from the shape of his footprints that he is a lizard. What name do you propose?”

I thought for a moment. “Boojum,” I said.

“Why? He is not a tree.”

I briefly summarized Carroll’s poem and explained the origin of the Boojum tree’s name. “So, I think Boojum is an appropriate name for this creature. If we come face to face with it in the open chaparral we might easily vanish—into its stomach.”

He nodded. “Okay; we will call him Boojum.”

“We can’t stay under this rock forever, you know. Eventually we will have to confront the Boojum; or else starve to death or die of thirst.”

He nodded. "Tonight I will find Boojum and see exactly what he is and who controls him."

"What if he kills you?"

"Then you must make it back to Bácum on your own. Can you do that?"

"I can find Bácum and the spring, since I have their coordinates. The Boojum, however, is an entirely different problem. He might ambush me before I can even get off a shot."

"I will seek out Boojum in the Otherworld."

"How? In a dream?"

"Not a dream; in a vision. I will ask Hikuri to help me." He reached under his shirt and pulled out a small cloth bag, hanging from a leather lanyard around his neck. From this he poured out a handful of dry peyote buttons, the size of nickels and quarters. "Hikuri will show me the Boojum."

"Who is Hikuri?"

"The Peyote-god, or as some prefer to call him, Mescal. He will show me."

"I hope Hikuri will also show you how to kill the Boojum," I said.

"Perhaps he will show me its weakness."

"If it has one," I said.

"Every creature has both strengths and weaknesses; even Wolf and Bear have weaknesses. They can be killed in spite of their great strength and cunning, if their weaknesses are understood."

"And if you have a big gun," I added.

"Oh, they can be killed in other ways as well. My ancestors killed them for thousands of years before there were any guns."

"That's true," I admitted. "However, I don't have the skills or experience to do such a thing."

"Nor I," he admitted. "But Hikuri will show me how to do whatever might be necessary."

"I hope you're right." I paused. "There's one other thing," I added.

"What is that?"

"There's probably more than one."

He thought about this for a moment and then nodded his head. "That would make sense. But I hope there is only one. One Boojum will be difficult enough."

"No kidding!" I thought. "We will soon run out of water," I said. "How far away is another spring?"

"The only one I know of is about an eight hour's walk to the east. But the Boojum needs water, too. So, there must be water nearby if he lives here. Perhaps we will be able to backtrack and find it if we run out of water."

Exhausted from our forced march I lowered my head and dropped off to sleep.

When I awoke there was significantly less light in our hiding space and I surmised that the sun had set. I checked my watch and found that I had been asleep for over two hours. I glanced over at Woi and saw that he appeared to be asleep as well, but then I noticed that he had spit out at least six masticated peyote buttons onto the ground in front of him. He had also thrown up his energy bar. I knew that peyote often caused nausea, though I had never used the drug myself. I tried to wake him, but he was totally unresponsive. It was obvious that he had passed into a deep trance, so deep that it was almost as if he was in a coma, and I had no doubt that he was presently wandering around somewhere in the Otherworld, hunting for Boojums.

A few minutes later I heard the Boojum for the first time. It was noisily sniffing the ground near the entrance to our hiding place. It could no doubt smell Woi's vomit. The sniffing and snorting were quite loud and it was obviously a large animal. I decided that it would have had no difficulty in killing a mere cow. It then began pawing and scraping at the entrance gap, trying to see if it was possible to enlarge the gap enough to reach in for us. I reached into my backpack and retrieved my handgun, a .357 magnum.

When I cocked the hammer the boojum heard the noise and bellowed; a terrifyingly loud, guttural roar that made the hair on the back of my neck stand up as it echoed off of the cliff walls in the canyon. I bent down and peered through the gap right into the bright red eye of a very large reptilian creature that looked for all the world like a velociraptor.

I decided that this might be the best chance I would ever have at a clear shot at the monster and I aimed my pistol at its eyeball, not three feet away, and pulled the trigger. The noise of the shot in the confined space was deafening and my ears instantly started ringing, but this was nothing compared to the scream that came from the Boojum. I glanced over at Woi and saw that he hadn't moved a muscle in spite of all of the noise. It made me wonder whether he might actually be dead. I slipped over and felt for his pulse, which was racing. He was obviously alive and very actively tripping through the Otherworldly tulips.

There was no doubt that I had hit the Boojum; I couldn't have missed at point-blank range, and the impact of the bullet would have been enough to crack an engine block. I couldn't imagine that the Boojum could have survived such a hit, no matter how hard its head was. Nonetheless, I wasn't about to go outside and check its pulse. I could imagine being grabbed in the jaws of its mate as I struggled through the gap, even though I didn't know if there was more than one of them.

I decided to wait for Woi's return from the bright lights of Otherworld before doing anything. I scooted back over to my spot and waited. I took the time to remove the spent shell and replace it with a live round. After seeing the Boojum face to face I decided that I wanted to keep my weapon fully loaded.

Four hours later my ears were still ringing, and I was beginning to wonder if I might have done serious damage to my hearing. It was beginning to get on my nerves; like a telephone that won't quit ringing. About three hours later I finally managed to drift off back to sleep.

Morning finally came and the light coming into our hiding place eventually woke me up. I looked over at Woi and it appeared that he had fallen over. I reached back over and checked his pulse which was steadier now and not as fast. I assumed that he was probably making his way home. I moved back over to the gap and peered outside. I could see the body of the Boojum a little ways off from the entrance where it had landed. It wouldn't be long before vultures would be arriving.

About noon Woi stirred and managed to sit up with his back leaning against the rock wall and his head between his knees. It was obvious that he was still nauseated. I offered him a sip of water, which he took, but then started heaving, though his stomach was empty. I decided to leave him alone.

Two hours later he seemed to regain consciousness and looked over at me. "How long have I been out?" he asked in a very shallow voice.

"I'm not sure. About twelve hours, I guess. What did you learn?"

"We are under attack from a *bruja*. I have encountered her before on several occasions. She is very powerful and just as evil. Somehow she knows that we are searching for the little Boojum trees, though I have no idea how she came by this knowledge. Perhaps from a mouse in Miguel Martínez's shop in Sonoyta who overheard something while you were there, or possibly even a bird. She is trying to prevent us from going there. She is protecting the trees."

"Why would she care? I just want to see the plants, not harm them."

"She doesn't know this."

"Why would these trees be so special to her?"

"Their seeds are magical; stronger than mescal. They let one see clearly into the future. She wants these seeds for herself; only for herself."

I was skeptical, but decided not to express this. "The Boojum found us," I said.

"How do you know?"

"He appeared at the entrance. He could smell us. When I peered through the gap I looked him right in the eye; not three feet away. His eye was red."

"This is very serious," he said.

"I killed it," I said.

This news startled him. "How?"

I shot him point-blank in the eye with my pistol as he peered inside trying to see us. His body lies outside, covered in vultures who are busily feeding on his carcass."

"Are you serious?" he asked as he moved over to the entrance to see for himself. "Yes, I see him. Have you gone out to examine him?"

"No, I decided to wait for your return from the Otherworld before doing that. I am worried that it might have a mate, who will be very angry with us."

"So that's what happened in the vision!" he said.

"What do you mean? What did you see?"

He pulled back away from the opening and leaned back against the wall, obviously still groggy and nauseated. "I journeyed across the desert to the high mesa where the little Boojum trees grow, guided by Rabbit. The *bruja* was there along with two Boojums, one on either side of her."

I was confused. “Two Boojum trees?”

“No, not the trees—the lizard-creatures, like the one you killed. They tried to kill me, and I had to fight with them furiously for hours for my life, with all my skill and powers. At one point, just as I was in danger of being overwhelmed, one of the Boojums screamed and fell dead, wounded terribly in its eye. This frightened the *bruja*, who evidently assumed that I had somehow done this. She leapt atop the other Boojum’s back and they fled down the side of the mesa. This was obviously when you shot the Boojum that lies outside. You saved my life.”

“Were the little Boojum trees still there?”

“Yes. Remarkably, in my vision they were made of gold, surrounded by blue and purple auras. Their seeds sparkled like diamonds, both on the stalks and on the ground where they had fallen, creating kaleidoscopic beams of light as they swayed in the breeze that blew across the mesa. Ordinary Boojum trees do not exhibit these colorful aspects.”

“Well, the bad news in your vision is that the Boojum has a mate,” I observed.

“Yes. It does. It will be here soon, searching for us, if it is not here already. The Vultures will guide it. You were wise not to venture out alone. I will see what there is to see.”

He had no more said this than he vanished in the twinkling of an eye. I looked up just in time to see a small brown bat depart through an opening near the top of our hiding place.

Thirty-minutes later the bat returned and in an instant Woi was seated in the same place he had been, in the same position. Just like that: one moment he was there, the next he wasn’t; one moment he wasn’t there and the next moment he was. It was eerie and amazing.

“We should leave. The Boojum is approximately five miles away. She has seen the vultures. She could be here in twenty or thirty minutes.”

"Where will we go?"

"To the high mesa, of course. We will collect some seeds from the Boojum trees."

"But the Boojum—what about the Boojum? She will be on our trail and we cannot run ten miles an hour."

"She will be delayed when she finds her mate."

"How long?"

"I'm hoping for at least a few hours. That should be enough time."

"But even if we get to the trees first we will be too tired to run to some other shelter—if we can even find one."

"In the vision I saw the trees' location and a place to hide. We will be all right." He quit talking and got down on his stomach and slid out of the opening at the base of the enormous rock slab. I pushed my rifle and backpack through to him and wriggled my way out. The vultures took wing.

"Give me just a few minutes. I want to cut off a claw to take back," I said starting to remove the knife I wore on my belt from its sheath, "to prove that the Boojum exists. No one will believe me without it."

"No. Its mate would follow the scent like a beacon. Don't touch the carcass. Besides, no one will believe you, anyway, regardless."

I decided he was probably right. I estimated that the Boojum would have stood eight feet at the top of its head and was probably fifteen feet from its nose to the tip of its tail. The slug that I had put through its right eye had torn off most of the left-side of the skull when it exited. "Well," I said, "at least we know these things are mortal."

"Perhaps," he said.

"Perhaps? Look for yourself; it's dead. I blew half of its head away."

He ignored me. "We must hurry," he said and turned to go up the mountain.

"Wait," I said. "It will be easier to go downhill."

"That is where the Boojum is coming from. She will cut across our path and be on us before we can escape. We must go over the top. She is too large to go over and will have to circle around the mountain in order to cut across our path in order to find us again. We will save time. Perhaps at least an hour."

So, we went up. By the time we reached the plateau I was completely winded. Woi was waiting for me, not even breathing hard. He was looking at something in the distance. I came over to where he was, gulping for air. "There she is," he said, pointing to something that I couldn't see. "She is running along the riverbed." I fished a small pair of binoculars out of my pack and looked in the direction he indicated for a few moments before I could pick her up, a very small dot, moving surprisingly fast, perhaps twenty miles per hour.

Woi turned and headed across the small top of the mesa towards the opposite side.

I realized that I was a distinct liability for Woi in this increasingly desperate situation. Had he been alone he could have simply shape-shifted into a bat or a bird and flown away. End of problem. I now had no doubt that this was how he had survived decades alone in the desert. But I could not shape-shift into anything and was very vulnerable. His basic choices were to abandon me to my fate or remain in human form and try to get me to safety without being intercepted by the pursuing Boojum intent on terrible retribution.

Woi walked quickly back and forth along the edge of the mesa's caprock, searching for a way down the exposed cliffs, so that we would have a chance of descending without killing ourselves in the process. Finally he made a decision. "This way," he said. "Quickly."

He led the way over the edge, and I followed close behind so that I could see how he would manage the descent. A slip would mean a hundred-foot free fall down the shear face of the cliff and certain death against the jumble of boulders and rocks below. It took us twenty terrifying minutes to make it down from the top of the mesa to its sloped sides and another fifteen minutes down to the desert floor. We caught our breath and took a drink from a canteen. "This way," Woi said as he set off at a steady, fast pace, with me trying my best to keep up with the old man.

Woi stuck to animal trails and dry washes in order to avoid the worst of the cactus and thorn trees. It was indirect, but faster than it would have been to attempt to head straight through the thick chaparral. About noon we took a minor detour towards a verdant stand of palo verdes where Woi believed there would be water, and where we found a small spring. The water was rather bitter, but we had no choice as our canteen supply was getting low. About five p.m. Woi stopped and pointed to a small mesa in the distance. "That is the home of the little Boojum trees," he said.

I estimated that it was at least eight miles away. "We won't make it in time," I said. "It will take us at least another two hours to reach the mesa and darkness will overtake us. Without shelter for the night we will be easy pickings for the Boojum. The moon won't rise until about ten."

Woi didn't argue, but just stood there breathing hard to catch his breath, looking toward the little mesa on the horizon. Finally he pointed toward a rocky outcropping about half a mile off to our left, its sides studded with enormous clumps of Organ Pipe cactus. "We will go there," he decided. "Perhaps we can find shelter for you there."

This didn't sound very promising. "Perhaps?" I asked. I had gotten used to Woi knowing exactly where we were going; where there was water and where there was shelter.

"Yes, perhaps. I have never explored that place. But I don't have a better idea. All we need is a hole or a ledge big enough for you to hide in. I can find shelter in many places. A bat needs only an overhang and a tiny foothold." He obviously didn't want to argue anymore about it and turned towards the outcrop. "Pay special attention to the cactus," he warned. "We must make our way there without benefit of a pathway or trail."

He unsheathed his machete and began chopping his way through, lopping off sections of cholla and hacking away low branches of mesquite to create a path just wide enough to get through without being covered in spines or scratched into shreds. Things went well at first, but I eventually stumbled and instinctively reached out to catch myself and brushed against a stalk of cholla. It was a painful blunder and I would be spending a few hours later in the evening pulling out spines with the tweezers I had in my backpack—that was, of course, if I was still alive and not Boojum chow. Of all of the cacti, I hated the cholla the most. It seemed to leap at you if you even got close—intellectually I knew that this was impossible, but experience seemed to confirm its ability.

"Here!" Woi finally declared, pointing at the base of a particularly magnificent colony of ancient Organ Pipe cactus that seemed to have somehow embedded itself into a jagged pile of large boulders. "There is enough room for you to squeeze in at the base, in that crevice." He was pointing at a narrow slit. He cut a short path to this crevice. Let me use your light," he said. I retrieved a flashlight from out of my backpack and handed it to him. He then slithered inside head-first to check for rattlesnakes. He emerged in a few moments and said, "There are only a few snakes and they are harmless. You will be fine if you leave them alone. The big bull snake will give you a nasty bite if you grab him, but he is not venomous. Just leave him alone. He is in a back corner. The others will stay away from you."

"The others?"

"Only a dozen or so," he assured me. "Nothing to worry about. Rattlesnakes won't try to enter with the large bull snake inside. They fear him. He eats them." He helped me take off my backpack and held my rifle while I squirmed inside, feet first. Woi had made it look easy, but his midriff was considerably thinner than mine. My feet bumped up against a few snakes, which was unnerving. Woi then slipped my rifle and backpack inside to me. "Don't venture out unless I call you," he warned. "The Boojum may be near. I will find her and come back later to tell you." He then disappeared from my narrow view and I heard him sing a quiet chant as he went back down the slope. Then there was silence.

I got my pistol out of my backpack and had it at the ready. I then found the tweezers and set about slowly and methodically pulling needles out of my palm. An hour later Woi's face appeared at the crevice's opening. "Señor Rex. Are you there?"

I squirmed up a little to the opening and showed my face. "Yes."

"Have any of the snakes bitten you?"

"No, not yet. Do you have news of the Boojum?"

"She is about an hour away, though if she decided to run she could be here much sooner. It evidently took her quite a while to circle the mesa and cut back across our trail. She will soon be here, no doubt, and she will be looking for you."

"If she sticks her face into the crevice I may get a chance to shoot her."

"That would be fortunate, though I think you might not be so fortunate this time."

"Why?"

"The *bruja* will no doubt have warned her not to do this."

"Really?"

"Yes."

"What will you do?"

"I will go to the mesa and collect the seeds of the small Boojum tree. They will show me the future and I will then know what to do. I have asked Javelina to stand guard here. You may see him now and then. He is your protector. Do not shoot at him. If you hear him squeal loudly then you will know that the Boojum is nearby."

"What if she kills him?"

"She may try, but I am confident that Javelina will be safe. He is very quick and can move easily through the cacti. The Boojum cannot."

He turned and left without further word. I listened as he made his way back down the slope. Five minutes later a javelina boar with fearsome tusks appeared at the opening to my hiding place. He snuck his snout into the crevice opening and grunted softly, as if reassuring me, and then moved away. I pulled myself as far back into the crevice as I could manage, my innate fear of snakes having abated significantly in the face of the Boojum's imminent arrival. About twenty minutes later I heard the javelina squeal, followed by a bone-chilling roar from the Boojum. I hoped that this was just the javelina's signal and not that the Boojum had somehow managed to harm him, in spite of Woi's confidences.

A few minutes later I saw the Boojum as she came up the pathway that Woi had cleared. I picked up my pistol and fired, but missed. The Boojum bolted to the right. I cursed myself for being overly anxious to shoot. I should have waited.

A few minutes later she walked across the opening and I got a clear view of the razor-sharp hinged claws. They were terrifying. Images of her using them to tear me apart rushed through my mind. I cocked the pistol and aimed it at the opening, ready to shoot if she lowered her head and peered into the crevice. I could hear her sniffing for me and it was obvious that she knew where I was; perhaps she could smell fear. But she didn't show her face and I suspected that Woi was right; that the *bruja* had warned her.

During the next few hours she occasionally stepped in front of the opening her huge feet kicking tiny gravel into by face. Every now and then the javelina would squeal to remind me that she was still near and the Boojum would angrily roar back at him. Once I heard her chase after him, crashing through the cacti.

I finally decided to shoot her in the foot, reasoning that, if nothing else, it would slow her down if she came after us when we would have to make a run for Bácum. I pulled the trigger at the next opportunity and the bullet shattered the bones in one of her ankles, spraying me with a fine mist of Boojum blood. She roared in surprise and pain and the javelina squealed, no doubt frightened by the unexpected pistol's report. The Boojum stumbled and crashed through the cacti as she rolled down the hillside. I hoped that she was now covered in cholla spines. It would serve her right.

Once again my ears were ringing. If the javelina squealed I could no longer hear him. I wanted very much to see how badly the Boojuim was injured, but I knew that it would be very foolhardy to venture out. It was very unlikely that the wound to her foot had killed her and she would almost certainly be nearby and very, very angry.

At twilight most of the snakes, including the huge bull snake, a striking specimen that was at least eight feet long, thankfully left to hunt. A little while later darkness engulfed everything. About three hours later still the full moon finally rose and I could once again see out the opening, though there was nothing to see but the indigo sky and a few twinkling stars. I began to worry about Woi. How would he get back to me without encountering the wounded Boojum?

I eventually drifted off to a fitful sleep. I was awakened by Woi's quiet voice, "Señor Rex?"

I pulled myself up to the opening. "Yes."

"Are you all right?"

"Yes. I shot the Boojum in the ankle."

"Yes, I know. But she is still very much alive."

"Where is she?"

"I left her back on the mesa with the little Boojum trees."

"What is she doing over there?"

"Hunting for me."

"Won't she just track you back here?"

"I flew off of the top of the mesa. She will not be able to track me."

"As a bat, I suppose."

"No. I flew as Raven."

"I'm curious. Why as a raven?"

"I had to carry these." He reached inside his shirt and produced the little peyote bag, which he opened and from which he poured seeds into his palm. They looked vaguely familiar.

"Seeds from the dwarf Boojum tree?"

"Yes."

"That's great!" I said, but he could tell I was nonetheless disappointed.

"What is it, señor Rex?"

"I had hoped to see the trees."

"It is far too dangerous. It would probably cost you your life. I will give you some of these seeds. You can plant them and watch them grow in your own garden someday."

"You're right. I certainly don't want to feed the Boojum."

"You are still in great danger. She will eventually come back here looking for you. You have slowed her down a little, but that is all. She ignores pain. She is very powerful, and equally determined."

He turned and headed back down the hillside. I followed. "How about the javelina?" I asked. "Is he safe?"

"Yes; he is safe. He is very quick."

"Please thank him for me," I said.

"I will."

I gave Woi a drink and we set out back to where we had come from. We stopped about noon to rest and eat some more of my dwindling supply of energy bars. While I rested Woi got up and said, "I will see where the Boojum is. Stay here. Have your rifle ready in case she is closer than we think."

He went back down the wash and disappeared. A few moments later I saw a raven fly away, back in the direction from which we had come.

Twenty minutes later Woi reemerged from the chaparral and came over to where I was seated. "She has picked up our trail again. She is walking and not running, since her foot is injured. But she could be here in another few hours; three at the most. We should go. With luck we can be back at our earlier shelter before she catches up."

We jogged the last two miles around the mesa rather than go up and over, which was a dangerous and arduous climb. We were both out of breath by the time we arrived at the huge rock slab, frightening away a few vultures who were still picking at what little remained of the first Boojum, which was now little more than skin and bone. I took the rifle and climbed up onto a large boulder to see if I could spot her approach. About fifteen minutes later I saw her, following our trail. I took a shot at her from a distance of about 150 yards when she passed through a dry wash river bed that afforded a clear view, but unfortunately I hadn't led her enough and only managed to hit her tail. The impact knocked her down, but she scrambled up and dove into the chaparral. I decided that it was time to get back under the rock and scurried down. We both slipped inside and waited. I had my pistol ready in case she showed herself at the entrance, but she was now much too wary.

Completely exhausted and still winded, we both drifted off to sleep a few minutes later. Much later, I awoke in pitch blackness and checked my watch. It was about 9:30. "Woi?" I said aloud. There was no response. I fumbled around in my backpack and retrieved my flashlight and found that he was gone. About twenty-minutes later the moon rose again and about an hour later I heard a bat enter through the small gap in the rock above. Woi suddenly reappeared, sitting where I had last seen him. Even though I had seen this happen before it was still startling and hard to get used to.

"Did you find her?" I asked.

"Yes. She is waiting for us down at the bottom of the arroyo."

"What shall we do?"

"I don't know. I will eat one of the Boojum tree seeds to see if it will show me the future."

"Have you ever experimented with a Boojum tree seed?"

"No," he admitted.

"What if it is lethally poisonous?"

"Then I may die. But I doubt that there is enough poison in just one little seed to kill a full-grown man."

"The seeds of some plants can easily kill a man. Even a small piece of a castor bean can kill. Have you ever seen an animal or bird eat a Boojum tree seed?"

"No," he admitted.

"Then I think that it's too high a risk," I argued.

"Staying under this rock is a high risk. The Boojum is waiting for us to emerge and she is a very high risk—especially to you."

"I have another idea. I know that you can shape-shift at will. What if I climb up to a high vantage point with my rifle—high enough so that I have a clear view of the area just below us. If you go out and attract the Boojum's attention it will surely try to attack you. You can then escape at the last minute—fly away as a bat or a raven—and I will shoot the Boojum."

"There is a risk that you might miss and shoot me."

"No, I am a better shot than that."

"All right. We can try your plan. We will wait until morning when you can see well."

We went back to sleep. When it was morning Woi flew out again to see where the Boojum was. "She has not moved," he said on his return. "She still waits at the mouth of the arroyo. She is patient."

"Good. I will find a spot to shoot from. You can pass the rifle up to me when I am in position."

There was a large boulder nearby that I thought I could successfully climb and went up. Woi handed me the rifle. "All right," I said. "I'm ready whenever you are. Don't go down too far. Not more than seventy yards. I don't want the shot to be too difficult."

Woi walked a little ways down and began singing a chant in a loud voice. I recognized it as a part of the accompaniment for the Deer Dance. The Boojum cautiously appeared within a few minutes, a few hundred yards further down the arroyo, peeking out from behind a large mesquite. When she clearly saw Woi, she charged, surprisingly fast considering the damage to her ankle. Woi acted as if he was unaware of her and continued to chant. I took careful aim and when she was no more than twenty yards from him I fired. The bullet, which struck her in the chest, dropped her instantly. Woi never bothered to shape-shift, but stood still to look at her. When the Boojum lifted her head slightly I put a second bullet into her skull.

Woi walked back up to where I was standing on top of the boulder. "You are an excellent shot, though I think that perhaps you waited a little too long to fire." I handed the rifle down to him and climbed down. We both went back to the creature and studied her. I was amazed that she had been able to walk on her injured foot, which was a mess and was now obviously infected. The pain must have been unimaginable. The final shot had blown away the back of her skull.

I went back to our hiding place and retrieved my backpack and went back down to the carcass. I removed a claw with my hunting knife as a trophy and tucked it away inside the pack. We then set off to find the spring where we had spent our first night.

That night, as we sat by the spring, eating a meal of jerky, we were finally able to relax. The sky was a clear powder blue and the temperature was mild. We were both physically and mentally exhausted, but happy to still be alive.

After the meal Woi removed the little bag of seeds from under his shirt and counted out twelve seeds, which he gave to me. I put them in a plastic baggie and stuffed them into a side pocket on my pack for safe keeping. He then took another seed from the pouch and before I could protest, popped it into his mouth, chewed it briefly and then swallowed it, followed by a drink of water. He closed the pouch, slipped it back under his shirt and then laid down beside the spring to wait for whatever might happen. He shuddered, as if experiencing a mild seizure, jerked several times and then lost consciousness. His breathing became shallow—almost imperceptible—and I began to worry that he might have died of respiratory arrest.

I sat beside him, checking his pulse every now and then and guarding him from whatever might decide to come up to the water in the pool. At times his pulse raced wildly. At other times it dropped dangerously low. He was obviously experiencing a wild trip in the Otherworld.

Twelve hours later he stirred and began to struggle as if fighting to regain consciousness. I had no idea how to help him. After another half-hour he finally managed to open an eye and with great effort sat up. I offered him a drink, but he waved it away. He rested his head between his knees and took deep breaths. Finally, after another hour he was able to talk, though his words were slurred.

At first I couldn't understand what he was saying and I struggled to make any sense out of his garbled speech. Then it finally dawned on me what he was trying to say: "There are more than two," were his ominous words.

Somehow this possibility hadn't occurred to me. I had assumed only a mating pair.

Again I had no idea what to do. The only safe shelter I knew of was back where we had come from that morning. Bácum was an equal distance away. Woi was so sick and groggy from his Otherworldly trip that he could not even stand, much less take a long hike. The ledge fifty feet above the spring where we had slept the first night was a possibility, but I would have to wait for him to regain enough strength to climb up there on his own. I certainly couldn't carry him up there on my back. I felt helpless, and could do nothing but wait for him to regain his strength and better clarity of mind.

I retrieved my pistol, checked to be sure it was fully loaded, and waited. Night engulfed us, and I continued to wait, my anxiety building. Then the night noises began: a night bird's song; a rush of small footsteps scurrying through the dry brush; a sudden whirr of wings; a coyote's howl in the distance, somewhere off to the southeast; an owl's hoot. Everything startled me in the darkness, and every noise caused me to instinctively swing the pistol in that direction. I longed for the moonrise. Woi, dazed by the effect of the Boojum seed, still barely moved. He was obviously still tripping. Was he fighting for his life with the *bruja*? I wondered. Was he seeing the future, as he had hoped? Was he lost in some unfamiliar section of an Otherworldly desert?

Was he talking with Hikuri? Was he meeting his long-dead Yaqui ancestors? Anything seemed possible in the darkness.

Finally, the moon rose, still almost full, bathing the desert in an eerie, faintly luminescent light. The Boojum trees and Saguaro looked like elaborate black cardboard cutouts, their arms like the wild gestures of dancers frozen in time. I stared at the moon and finally made out the winged, turtle-headed Boojum sneaking up behind the hapless Baker to bite his neck.

A sudden loud squeal startled me so badly that I involuntarily pulled off a shot, the loud report echoing across the desert. It might as well have been a howitzer in the stillness. I was furious with myself; if there was a Boojum anywhere within miles it now knew where we were. A javelina boar appeared a few feet away, and I finally recognized him as Woi's protector. He had obviously squealed a warning that a Boojum was close by. He grunted softly and scurried away into the chaparral, disappearing around a thick clump of yucca. The gunshot even seemed to bring Woi a little ways out of his drugged stupor; as if he too was trying to home in on the noise. He said something in Yaqui, which I could not understand, then something else in unintelligibly slurred Spanish, followed by something equally unintelligible in Nahuatl. I was on the verge of panic. I pushed Woi's head back and threw water in his face, trying to bring him to. I slapped his face several times, which caused him to shake his head, obviously trying to clear his mind.

I placed my hands on his shoulders and shook him hard, which seemed to bring him a little further out of his drug-induced fog. "What?" he said in Spanish.

"We are in danger. We need to get up to the ledge. Can you get up?"

He struggled to his feet, using me as a brace. "Where?" he asked, still obviously confused. I turned him and pointed him in the direction we needed to go; up the steep side of the slope. I pushed and shoved, trying to help him climb. We almost fell back several times. Halfway up the slope my rifle slipped off of my shoulder and fell off into the brush. There was no way I could retrieve it without Woi falling, so I let it be. I would try to find it later, if we survived. With all of my strength I finally got Woi up onto the lip of the ledge, where a rattler was waiting, coiled to strike, his tail buzzing furiously. I blew him away with a single pistol shot. With my last bit of strength I climbed over Woi's limp body and drug him up onto the middle of the ledge.

The javelina squealed again, though this time is was a terrible scream, and then sudden silence. I knew without seeing that the Boojum had managed to kill him. This time he hadn't been quite quick enough.

For the next twenty minutes the Boojum struggled to climb up the steep hillside to where we were perched. It would manage to get about halfway up, then slip as it lost its footing and fall, crashing and tumbling down into the cacti. I kept hoping that it would break its neck, though I realized this was highly unlikely.

Two hours later Woi finally regained his senses and shook his head one final time to clear out the remaining cobwebs. "Where are we?" he asked.

"On the ledge above the spring where we came the first day."

"How did I get up here?"

"It took the two us. Frankly, we are lucky to be alive. We almost fell to our deaths several times as I pushed and shoved you. You did all you could do for yourself in the terrible state you were in. That was two hours ago."

"Why are we up here?"

"A Boojum awaits below at the pool."

"Are you sure?"

"Yes. Javelina came and warned us. Soon after we managed to get up here the Boojum spent twenty minutes trying to climb after us. It finally gave up." I paused. "I'm afraid that I have some bad news. It killed Javelina. I heard Javelina's death-scream. It gave its life trying to protect us."

He seemed stunned by this terrible news. "This is bad. He was my friend."

"I know; and mine. I'm sorry."

I gave him a few minutes to process this news.

"When you tried to come out of your trip you were very ill and you had a very hard time coming back to this world. How are you feeling? I was getting very worried about you."

"I feel much better now. The seed was very powerful; too powerful. I am used to taking heavy doses of peyote, but this was so much stronger! I should have only taken half of the seed; perhaps even less. One seed has the power of fifteen old peyote buttons. It would be very dangerous for novices."

"You had hoped to see the future? Did you?"

"Yes."

I waited for him to tell me something about what he had seen, but it wasn't forthcoming. Finally I asked him outright, "What did you see?"

He didn't respond at first. "What I saw is very difficult to describe. It was terrifying. I will try to tell you, though words are not adequate. I was high up, flying like the Eagle and could see for many, many miles. A bright, burning star, trailing smoke, fell into the desert and exploded. Everything died and burned up: all peoples; all animals; all plants; everything. Even the air itself burned."

"When will this happen?"

"I don't know."

"Not exactly; just approximately. Soon? In the distant future?"

"I don't know."

"What about the Boojums?"

"They were consumed as well. Everything vanished or was burned—except perhaps the rocks and dirt—following a brilliant flash of light."

"What about Hikuri? Did you speak with him?"

"He too was consumed in the fireball. Everything vanished. Even he could not stop it, though he tried."

I didn't know what to say for a while. "Is there anything you can do to stop this from happening?"

"No."

"Is there anything *anyone* can do to stop it from happening?"

"I don't know. I cannot imagine what anyone could do."

"In your vision, did you see us getting back to Bácum?"

"Bácum also vanished in the fireball. All of the people and buildings; even the church."

"Only Bácum?"

"No; all of the cities in Sonora as far as I could see. No one survived."

"And in the United States as well?"

"I don't know. That is too far away. I couldn't see how far the wall of fire traveled. It spread like a wave in a pond when a stone is thrown into it. Outward, like an expanding circle, consuming everything in its path."

It was obvious from his description of the vision that the active alkaloids in the Boojum tree seeds were powerful psychotropic substances and capable of producing vivid hallucinations and visions.

"Have you ever watched television?" I asked him.

"Yes. Two times while I was in Guadalupe."

"What did you see?"

"A football game and a cartoon about a hideous creature named SpongeBob."

"That's it?"

"Yes. Those are the only two things I have seen. I do not like the television. I prefer to watch my dreams and visions sent by Mescal."

"Never a program about asteroids or space travel?"

"No."

"Any stories about space travel or nuclear war?"

"No. Only the football game and the Sponge Bob. I told you this. Why do you keep asking?"

"What you described in your vision sounds very much like the impact of a large asteroid hitting the earth."

"What is an asteroid?"

"It is a huge rock from outer space, perhaps as large as a several miles across. If it hits the earth then it will cause a huge explosion, much like that you have described. I was wondering if you were simply remembering something you saw on television. Perhaps on a nature channel."

"No. I have described something that I have seen in a vision—my vision—not the tele's vision."

"Thank you for sharing your vision with me. I don't think that I ever want to eat the seed of the Boojum tree."

He nodded. "You are wise. It would surely kill you; you might never come back. I am experienced with peyote and I almost did not make it back. At one point I was falling into blackness when I heard an explosion in the distance. I fought my way back to the sound."

"What shall we do about the Boojum?"

"Can you shoot it?"

"I doubt it. I dropped my rifle in trying to get you up here onto the ledge. All I have now is this pistol. It is powerful enough to kill it, but it is difficult to hit anything unless it is close."

"Then we shall have to trick the Boojum into coming in close. We will do that when the sun rises. I am sleepy now."

He stretched out along the ledge and was asleep within seconds.

When the sun's rays struck Woi's face he awoke and sat up. I was already awake, looking over the edge. "Can you see the Boojum?" he asked.

"Yes. He is there, about a hundred yards away; near that large velvet mesquite. He is too far away for me to hit with accuracy."

"I will go and get him," he said and then vanished. A small brown bat flew a tight circle then dove towards the pool. Woi suddenly reappeared beside the pool. He bent down and took a drink, then stood up and yelled at the Boojum in Yaqui. I had no idea what he said, but the Boojum seemed to understand and instantly charged. When it was no more than twenty yards from him Woi shape-shifted into a raven and flew out of harm's way. He repeatedly dove at the Boojum's head, tormenting it into a rage, always just out of reach. Finally the raven flew up and landed on the ledge. Suddenly Woi reappeared, laughing loudly at the Boojum, taunting it. It roared and scrambled up the slope again, determined to reach the ledge.

Woi turned to me and said, "I think you can hit it now."

I crept over to the edge and quickly put two bullets into its head. It crumpled without so much as a growl and slipped back down toward the pool, finally bumping up against a large Joshua Tree, knocking it over.

"Good," Woi said. "Now we should go to Bácum. Let's see if we can find your rifle before we go. There is no telling how many more of these things are searching for us."

My heart sunk at the thought that there might actually be more of them.

We made our way down and located the rifle, which was ruined, having obviously been stepped on. The stock was splintered and the barrel bent. We filled our canteens and left.

Fortunately there were no more Boojums and we finally walked into Bácum late in the afternoon. To my surpise, my rental SUV was still there. We went over to it and I lifted up the carpet on the passenger side and retrieved the $500 that I had hidden there. I handed the money to Woi. "Here is our agreed price," I said.

"But you never saw the Boojum trees! You owe me nothing."

"Nonsense! I owe you my life—many times over. And you have given me the seeds. I will plant them and I will yet see these trees."

He shrugged. "Are you sure, señor Rex?"

"Yes. It's been fascinating to get to know you. I wish you well."

"And you, señor. Perhaps I will see you again sometime. I will try to visit you in ten years and see if your little Boojum trees have survived."

"Good. I will be looking for you. But come to the door. You needn't go down the chimney."

He smiled.

It was about ten years later and I was in my backyard on Christmas Eve, tending to my small collection of desert plants in the balmy winter sunshine. In one corner, next to my ordinary Boojum tree, which had grown a few feet taller over the past decade, were three two-foot tall dwarf Boojums that had sprouted from the seeds that Woi had collected on our Sonoran expedition. I had placed a plastic Rudolph reindeer yard ornament, with a red light for a nose, next to them to celebrate the season. I never told anyone about the uniqueness of the small Boojums, but rather described them as being rather stunted, hoping that this would discourage any thoughts of sneeking in some dark night and taking them. There was a big demand for desert plants and it was common enough for a rare specimen to simply disappear from your yard.

I had never experimented with taking a bite of a dwarf Boojum seed, though I had licked one of them once. I had immediately seen flashes of intense color and that had been enough for me.

As I puttered around I glanced up and noticed an old acquaintance, a raven, perched atop the cinderblock wall that surrounded my backyard and provided some privacy. You might think that a raven is a raven and that they all look alike, but that is far from the truth; this was the one that had led me into the desert to meet Woi.

"*Feliz Navidad*, Raven," I said. "We meet again!"

The large bird lifted off of the wall and landed in front of the dwarf Boojums. The next moment Woi was standing there, studying the plants. "They look well," he said, then turned to me. "How are you doing, señor Rex?"

"I'm well, Woi, and you?"

"I too am well. Have you tried the seeds?"

"No, though I did lick one years ago to see how it tasted. I instantly saw bright colors dancing before my eyes. It was enough. I would never eat one. I'm afraid of them."

"You are wise to be afraid. They are too powerful."

"And you? Have you tried them again?"

"A few times. I now cut each seed into three pieces and take only one small piece. Even that small part is powerful enough."

"Do they show you the future?"

He shrugged. "Yes and no. I see things, but I have no way of knowing when they will happen."

"Could I ask you something I've wondered about for a long time?"

"Of course."

"Were you the raven who met me at the church in Bácum and led me into the desert?"

He smiled. "Yes. I wanted to study you, to see if I wanted to travel with you into the desert?"

I nodded. "What of the Boojums?"

"I have never encountered them again. I went back to where you had killed them—to each place—but their remains had vanished. It was as if they had never existed."

"They seemed very real at the time!"

"Yes, they were very real. Sometimes it is hard to distinguish things of this world from things of the Otherworld. Both are real. Sometimes they crisscross the boundaries. Sometimes they enter this world, but can't get back. The same thing can happen to people who travel into the Otherworld. It is a dangerous journey."

"I have something to show you. Please come inside."

I led the way through the kitchen and into my study. I opened a locked cabinet and took out a small chest and unlocked it. "Do you remember that I removed the claw from one of the Boojums?"

"Yes, I remember."

"I still have it. I keep it in here."

Woi's eyebrows went up in surprise. "Really?"

"Yes. I looked at it a few months ago." I opened the lid and to my dismay it was gone. "No!"

Woi smiled. "Now every trace of the Boojums is gone. I would have been amazed if you still had the claw."

I sat down on the sofa, exasperated at my obvious loss. "Perhaps I have had a burglar," I suggested.

Woi shook his head. "No, señor Rex, the claw has also returned to the Otherworld along with all of the other bones."

"What of your vision of the fallen star?" I asked. "Have you seen the vision again?"

He shook his head. "Thankfully, no! I hope that I never see such a terrifying thing again. It still haunts me day and night."

We walked back out into the garden. A few seconds later there was an intensely bright flash in the southern sky when a previously unidentified dark, M-type asteroid, nearly two miles in diameter, smashed into the Sonora Desert south of Sonoyta at over 30,000 miles per hour. Woi's eyes went wide in panic. I had no idea what was wrong.

"The star!" he whispered. "It has fallen!"

"What star?"

"The one in my vision! We are doomed!" A moment later Raven took wing, flying north as fast as his strong black wings could carry him. Unfortunately, it wasn't nearly fast enough. A few minutes later a towering wall of fire swept across Tucson at nearly the speed of sound.

For the star *was* a Boojum, you see.

Alice's Adventures in Wonderland, by Lewis Carroll 2008

Through the Looking-Glass and What Alice Found There,
by Lewis Carroll 2009

A New Alice in the Old Wonderland,
by Anna Matlack Richards, 2009

New Adventures of Alice, by John Rae, 2010

Alice Through the Needle's Eye, by Gilbert Adair, 2012

Wonderland Revisited and the Games Alice Played There,
by Keith Sheppard, 2009

Alice's Adventures under Ground, by Lewis Carroll 2009

The Nursery "Alice", by Lewis Carroll 2010

The Hunting of the Snark, by Lewis Carroll 2010

The Haunting of the Snarkasbord, by Alison Tannenbaum,
Byron W. Sewell, Charlie Lovett, and August A. Imholtz, Jr, 2012

Snarkmaster, by Byron W. Sewell, 2012

In the Boojum Forest, by Byron W. Sewell, 2014

Murder by Boojum, by Byron W. Sewell, 2014

Alice's Adventures in Wonderland,
Retold in words of one Syllable by Mrs J. C. Gorham, 2010

𐐈𐑊𐐮𐑅'𐑆 𐐈𐐼𐑂𐐯𐑌𐐽𐐲𐑉𐑆 𐐮𐑌 𐐎𐐲𐑌𐐼𐐲𐑉𐑊𐐰𐑌𐐼,
Alice printed in the Deseret Alphabet, 2014

Also available from **Evertype**

Alice printed in the Ewellic Alphabet, 2013

Alis'z Advenčrz in Wundrland,
Alice printed in the Ñspel orthography, 2014

Alice printed in the Nyctographic Square Alphabet, 2011

Alice printed in the Shaw Alphabet, 2013

ALISIZ ADVENCRZ IN WUNDRLAND,
Alice printed in the Unifon Alphabet, 2014

Behind the Looking-Glass: Reflections on the Myth of Lewis Carroll, by Sherry L. Ackerman, 2012

Clara in Blunderland, by Caroline Lewis, 2010

Lost in Blunderland: The further adventures of Clara, by Caroline Lewis, 2010

John Bull's Adventures in the Fiscal Wonderland, by Charles Geake, 2010

The Westminster Alice, by H. H. Munro (Saki), 2010

Alice in Blunderland: An Iridescent Dream, by John Kendrick Bangs, 2010

Rollo in Emblemland, by J. K. Bangs & C. R. Macauley, 2010

Gladys in Grammarland, by Audrey Mayhew Allen, 2010

Alice's Adventures in Pictureland, by Florence Adèle Evans, 2011

Eileen's Adventures in Wordland, by Zillah K. Macdonald, 2010

Phyllis in Piskie-land, by J. Henry Harris, 2012

Alice in Beeland, by Lillian Elizabeth Roy, 2012

The Admiral's Caravan, by Charles Edward Carryl, 2010

Davy and the Goblin, by Charles Edward Carryl, 2010

Alix's Adventures in Wonderland:
Lewis Carroll's Nightmare, by Byron W. Sewell, 2011

Álobk's Adventures in Goatland, by Byron W. Sewell, 2011

Alice's Bad Hair Day in Wonderland,
by Byron W. Sewell, 2012

The Carrollian Tales of Inspector Spectre,
by Byron W. Sewell, 2011

Alice's Adventures in An Appalachian Wonderland,
Alice in Appalachian English, 2012

Alice tu Vãsilia ti Ciudii, *Alice* in Aromanian, 2014

Alison's Jants in Ferlieland, *Alice* in Ayrshire Scots, 2014

Алесіны прыгоды ў Цудазем'і, *Alice* in Belarusian, 2013

Alice's Mishanters in e Land o Farlies,
Alice in Caithness Scots, 2014

Crystal's Adventures in A Cockney Wonderland,
Alice in Cockney Rhyming Slang, 2014

Alys in Pow an Anethow, *Alice* in Cornish, 2009

Alices Hændelser i Vidunderlandet, *Alice* in Danish, 2015

La Aventuroj de Alicio en Mirlando,
Alice in Esperanto, by E. L. Kearney, 2009

La Aventuroj de Alico en Mirlando,
Alice in Esperanto, by Donald Broadribb, 2012

Trans la Spegulo kaj kion Alico trovis tie,
Looking-Glass in Esperanto, by Donald Broadribb, 2012

Les Aventures d'Alice au pays des merveilles,
Alice in French, 2010

Alice's Abenteuer im Wunderland, *Alice* in German, 2010

Alice's Adventirs in Wunnerlaun,
Alice in Glaswegian Scots, 2014

Nā Hana Kupanaha a ʻĀleka ma ka ʻĀina Kamahaʻo,
Alice in Hawaiian, 2012

Ma Loko o ke Aniani Kū a me ka Mea i Loaʻa iā ʻĀleka ma Laila, *Looking-Glass* in Hawaiian, 2012

Aliz kalandjai Csodaországban, *Alice* in Hungarian, 2013

Eachtraí Eilíse i dTír na nIontas,
Alice in Irish, by Nicholas Williams, 2007

Lastall den Scáthán agus a bhFuair Eilís Ann Roimpi,
Looking-Glass in Irish, by Nicholas Williams, 2009

Eachtra Eibhlís i dTír na nIontas,
Alice in Irish, by Pádraig Ó Cadhla, 2014

Le Avventure di Alice nel Paese delle Meraviglie,
Alice in Italian, 2010

L's Aventuthes d'Alice en Êmèrvil'lie, *Alice* in Jèrriais, 2012

L'Travèrs du Mitheux et chein qu'Alice y dêmuchit, *Looking-Glass* in Jèrriais, 2012

Las Aventuras de Alisia en el Paiz de las Maraviyas, *Alice* in Ladino, 2014

Alisis pīdzeivuojumi Breinumu zemē, *Alice* in Latgalian, 2014

Alicia in Terra Mirabili, *Alice* in Latin, 2011

Alisa-ney Aventuras in Divalanda, *Alice* in Lingua de Planeta (Lidepla), 2014

La aventuras de Alisia en la pais de mervelias, *Alice* in Lingua Franca Nova, 2012

Alice ẹhr Ẹventüürn in't Wunnerland, *Alice* in Low German, 2010

Contoyrtyssyn Ealish ayns Çheer ny Yindyssyn, *Alice* in Manx, 2010

Dee Erläwnisse von Alice em Wundalaund, *Alice* in Mennonite Low German, 2012

The Aventures of Alys in Wondyr Lond, *Alice* in Middle English, 2013

L'Aventuros de Alis in Marvoland, *Alice* in Neo, 2013

Ailice's Anters in Ferlielann, *Alice* in North-East Scots, 2012

Die Lissel ehr Erlebnisse im Wunnerland, *Alice* in Palantine German, 2013

Соня въ царствѣ дива: Sonja in a Kingdom of Wonder, *Alice* in Russian, 2013

Ia Aventures as Alice in Daumsenland, *Alice* in Sambahsa, 2013

'O Tāfaoga a 'Ālise i le Nu'u o Mea Ofoofogia,
Alice in Samoan, 2013

Eachdraidh Ealasaid ann an Tìr nan Iongantas,
Alice in Scottish Gaelic, 2012

Alice's Adventirs in Wonderlaand, *Alice* in Shetland Scots, 2012

Alice Munyika Yamashiripiti, *Alice* in Shona, 2014

Ailice's Àventurs in Wunnerland,
Alice in Southeast Central Scots, 2011

Alices Äventyr i Sagolandet, *Alice* in Swedish, 2010

Ailis's Anterins i the Laun o Ferlies,
Alice in Synthetic Scots, 2013

'Alisi 'i he Fonua 'o e Fakaofo', *Alice* in Tongan, 2014

Alice's Carrànts in Wunnerlan, *Alice* in Ulster Scots, 2013

Der Alice ihre Obmteier im Wunderlaund,
Alice in Viennese German, 2012

Ventürs jiela Lälid in Stunalän, *Alice* in Volapük, 2014

Lès-avirètes da Alice ô payis dès mèrvèyes,
Alice in Walloon, 2012

Anturiaethau Alys yng Ngwlad Hud, *Alice* in Welsh, 2010

Di Avantures fun Alis in Vunderland, *Alice* in Yiddish, 2014

U-Alice Ezweni Lezimanga, *Alice* in Zulu, 2014

www.ingramcontent.com/pod-product-compliance
Ingram Content Group UK Ltd.
Pitfield, Milton Keynes, MK11 3LW, UK
UKHW041838190726
13854UKWH00002B/600